THE **MINI** ROUGH GUIDE TO
SCOTLAND

YOUR TAILOR-MADE TRIP
STARTS HERE

Tailor-made trips and unique adventures crafted by local experts

HOW ROUGHGUIDES.COM/TRIPS WORKS

STEP 1

Pick your dream destination, tell us what you want and submit an enquiry.

STEP 2

Fill in a short form to tell your local expert about your dream trip and preferences.

STEP 3

Our local expert will craft your tailor-made itinerary. You'll be able to tweak and refine it until you're completely satisfied.

STEP 4

Book online with ease, pack your bags and enjoy the trip! Our local expert will be on hand 24/7 while you're on the road.

PLAN AND BOOK YOUR TRIP AT
ROUGHGUIDES.COM/TRIPS

HOW TO DOWNLOAD
YOUR FREE EBOOK

1. Visit **www.roughguides.com/free-ebook** or scan the **QR code** opposite

2. Enter the code **scotland194**

3. Follow the simple step-by-step instructions

For troubleshooting contact: mail@roughguides.com

10 THINGS NOT TO MISS

8

9

10

A PERFECT DAY

9am

Breakfast. Kick off a day of culture with a traditional breakfast at the café inside the Scottish National Gallery of Modern Art before a look around the exhibition's collection of twentieth-century painting and sculpture.

10am

Edinburgh Castle. Follow the Mound, crossing Princes Street Gardens towards the Old Town and climb the steep steps up to the castle for fine views across the New Town.

11.30am

Castle Hill. Walk back down Castle Hill, passing attractions such as the Scotch Whisky Experience, Camera Obscura and Gladstone's Land, along the way. Take time to explore the vennels and wynds as you go.

12.30pm

Shopping. Visit Victoria Street, off George V Bridge, with its huddle of specialist shops, and the new St James Quarter just off Princes Street, before browsing the vintage stores, artisan food shops, independent boutiques and antiquarian bookshops clustered along Candlemaker Row, West Port and the Grassmarket.

1.30pm

Grassmarket. This thriving little market is packed with predominately artisan food sellers where you can pick up the likes of freshly baked bread, cheese and olives for picnics or delicious cooked meals such as paella. Retrace your steps and continue to High Street, where St Giles Cathedral dominates.

IN **EDINBURGH**

2pm

Royal Mile. Amble down the Royal Mile, ducking inside any of the big-hitters that catch your eye: the Museum of Childhood, John Knox House, the Museum of Edinburgh, Canongate Tolbooth. Near the end of the road, the Scottish Parliament building looms into view – an architectural one-off that still divides opinion. At the foot of the Royal Mile stands the Palace of Holyroodhouse.

3pm

Holyroodhouse. It is worth taking the time to see the fine collection of royal artefacts (if the royal family are not in residence); alternatively, if weather allows, explore the huge expanse of Holyrood Park behind.

4pm

Afternoon tea. Walk back up the Royal Mile. Just past the Scottish Parliament is *Clarinda's Tearoom*, a great pit stop to indulge in tea and home-baked treats.

7.30pm

Dinner. After freshening up at your hotel, head to the New Town – in and around George Street, good places to eat are endless. If Italian cooking is your preference, try the ever-popular *Gusto* or *Contini*.

9.30pm

On the town. You couldn't be in a better spot to finish the night in a chic bar or nightclub. On George Street, pop into *Copper Blossom* for cocktails or perhaps sip a Foxtrot Fizz or Red Rum at the *Bramble Bar* in nearby Queen Street.

CONTENTS

OVERVIEW

Scotland is a land steeped in romantic tradition. Its distinctive dress, its national drink, its famous bagpipe music and its stormy history give it an image recognisable worldwide. Though Scotland's territory is small, it has an unrivalled variety of landscape: deep green glens that slice through rugged mountains; forbidding castles reflected in dark, peat-stained lochs; moors awash with purple heather or yellow broom and gorse; green fields and hills dotted with sheep; and a wildly irregular coastline, incessantly pounded by the Atlantic and the North Sea, with both forbidding cliffs and sweeping sandy beaches.

Scotland's Highlands and Islands are a riot of spectacular natural beauty and one of the few remaining wilderness frontiers in all of Europe. Within easy reach of the cities of Edinburgh, Glasgow and Aberdeen are vast tracts of unspoiled country. You might see red deer break cover and golden eagles, or even an osprey, swooping overhead. In coursing streams, magnificent salmon and trout challenge the angler, while seals lounge on rocky shores. It's quite possible to walk all day and not see another human being.

The sea flows in to fill many of the country's three hundred lochs (except for the Lake of Menteith, Scots never call them 'lakes'); others are fresh water. The rolling hills and tranquil rivers of the south and the rich farmland of Fife and Royal Deeside present gentler but no less enticing landscapes.

The cultural mosaic, like the scenery, is hugely varied. Every summer Edinburgh, the intellectually and architecturally stimulating capital, is the scene of a distinguished international festival of music and the arts; and Glasgow is a former European City of Culture. Both cities have outstanding museums, and the Burrell Collection in Glasgow is one of Europe's great art galleries. All around the country you'll find theatre festivals, concerts, Highland gatherings, folk shows and crafts exhibitions. You can visit some 150 castles – some intact, others respectable ruins – while there are also baronial mansions, ancient abbeys and archaeological sites that invite exploration. The Gulf Stream along the west coast makes it possible for subtropical gardens to flourish, like those at Inverewe.

Stags in the Scottish Highlands

GEOGRAPHY AND CLIMATE

Covering the northernmost third of the United Kingdom, Scotland's 77,700 sq miles (30,000 sq km) are home to more than 5.4 million Scots, making up one-tenth of the total population of Great Britain. Scotland's territorial area includes 790 islands, of which 130 are inhabited. Many of these are popular tourist destinations easily reached by ferry or plane.

Happily, what people say about Scotland's weather isn't always true. Between May and October there are hours and even whole days of hot sunshine interrupting the rain, mist and bracing winds which perhaps keep the Scots so hardy. Interestingly enough, Scotland in an average year enjoys as much sun as London. Sightseers and photographers appreciate the amazing visibility to be had on clear days. Around lochs and on the west coast the only drawback is the midge, pesky biting flies that are impossible to avoid at the beginning and end of the day during the

Glen Coe

summer. The cold, snowy winters have made the Highlands Britain's skiing centre; there are many suitable areas for both downhill and cross-country skiing with Glen Coe having the steepest runs.

POLITICS

Constitutionally linked to England for nearly three centuries, Scotland is a land that keeps proudly unto itself. It prints its own bank notes (British versions circulate as well), and maintains independent educational and judicial systems, its own church, and more recently, its own Parliament. Gaelic is still spoken in the Western Highlands and Islands. This independent spirit has strengthened with the growth of the Scottish National Party (SNP) who instigated the 2014 referendum for independence and crushed the other parties in Scotland in the 2015, 2017 and 2019 general elections. Despite this surge of nationalism, the country is divided on whether to leave the United Kingdom and many of its citizens wish to remain in the union. And while the SNP are pushing for another vote on Scottish independence following the decision of the UK to leave the European Union (EU), the debate seems to have cooled for the time being.

TRUE GRIT

Over the centuries the hard-working Scots have made their mark on all corners of the globe: they were frontiersmen in North

America, explorers in Africa, pioneers in Australia. Nowadays, around ten times as many people of Scottish birth or ancestry live abroad as at home. Intellectually, the contribution made by Scots to world science, medicine and industry has been little short of astonishing. Above all, what binds the Scots together is a love of country plus a strong sense of community and national identity.

You'll meet with a friendly welcome almost everywhere you go: hospitality is an ancient Scottish tradition and its people are courteous and usually willing to go out of their way for you. All over Scotland you will see and hear the exhortation to 'Haste ye back' ('Come back soon'). After sampling the extraordinary beauty and diversity of this delightful country, you'll want to do just that.

KILTS AND TARTANS

Brightly coloured tartan kilts have been worn in the Highlands since the Middle Ages but most of the tartans we see today date from the early nineteenth century when the British royal family made the region fashionable. Daytime Highland dress consists of a knee-length kilt, matching waistcoat and tweed jacket, long knitted socks (with a *sgian-dubh* stuck in the right stocking), and flashes. A *sporran* (purse) hangs from the waist, and a plaid (sort of tartan rug) is sometimes flung over the shoulder. The Clearances in the aftermath of the Battle of Culloden in 1746 destroyed the clan system and Highland dress was forbidden. The kilt survived only because the Highland regiments, recruited to help defeat Napoleon, were allowed to continue to wear it. Authentic tartans are registered designs, and each clan had its own pattern. As the clans subdivided, many variations (setts) were produced. Today, there are some 2500 designs in all. To find out more, visit the Tartan Weaving Mill at 555 Castlehill, Edinburgh (open daily).

HISTORY AND CULTURE

Scotland's earliest settlers are thought to have been Celtic-Iberians who worked their way up from the Mediterranean – they have left us evidence of their presence in the cairns and standing stones which are found all over the country. In recent years, archaeologists discovered the remains of a huge timbered building west of Aberdeen which pre-dates Stonehenge by 1000 years.

By the time the Romans invaded Scotland in AD 84, the inhabitants of the northern region were the Picts, whom they dubbed 'the painted people'. The Roman legions defeated the Picts but were spread too thin to hold 'Caledonia', as they called the area. They withdrew behind the line of Hadrian's Wall, close to and south of the present Scottish-English border. The Picts left little evidence of their culture or language.

CHRISTIANITY AND THE NORSE INVASION

A Gaelic-speaking tribe from Ireland, the Scots founded a shaky kingdom in Argyll known as 'Dalriada'. In the late fourth century a Scot, St Ninian, travelled to Rome and, on his return, introduced Christianity to Dalriada. His colleague, St Mungo, established the foundation that is now the Cathedral of Glasgow. However, Christianity remained fairly isolated until the arrival in 563 of the great missionary from Ireland, St Columba. For more than thirty years, from the remote island of Iona, he spread the faith that would eventually provide the basis for the unification of Scotland. Tiny Iona today remains one of the most venerated sites in Christendom. In the late eighth century the Vikings swarmed over Europe setting up strongholds in the Orkneys and Hebrides and on the northern mainland. The Norsemen were to hold the Western Islands, Orkney and the Shetlands for hundreds of years.

UNIFICATION AND FEUDALISM IN THE SOUTH

The unifying influence of Christianity allowed an early chieftain, Kenneth MacAlpin, to unite the Scots and the Picts in 843. In 1018 this kingdom, led by Malcolm II, defeated the Northumbrians from the south at the Battle of Carham and extended its domain to the present southern boundary of Scotland. The 'murder most foul' of Malcolm's grandson, Duncan II, by Macbeth of Moray was the inspiration for Shakespeare's Scottish tragedy.

Malcolm III, also known as Malcolm Canmore, changed the course of Scottish history when he married an English princess in 1069. This was the highly pious Queen Margaret who was later canonised. She brought a powerful English influence to the Scottish scene and sought to implement a radical change, replacing the Gaelic-speaking culture of Scotland and its Celtic church with the English-speaking culture and institutions of the south and the church of Rome.

The rift that Margaret created was widened by her son, David I (reigned 1124–53). He embarked on a huge building programme, founding the great abbeys of Melrose and Jedburgh. He also brought Norman influence into Scotland and introduced to the Lowlands a French-speaking aristocracy and a feudal system of land ownership based on the Anglo-Norman model. He was not successful,

St Margaret's Chapel, Edinburgh

however, in imposing this system on the north, where the social structure was based on kinship and where the clan chieftain held land, not for himself, but for his people.

THE SHAPING OF SCOTLAND

The death of King Alexander III (1249–86) in a riding accident touched off a succession crisis that began what was to be the long, bloody struggle for Scottish independence. The English king, Edward I, was invited to arbitrate among the claimants to the throne. He seized his opportunity and installed John Balliol as his vassal king of Scots. But in 1295 Balliol renounced his fealty to Edward and allied himself with France. In retaliation the English king sacked the burgh of Berwick, crushed the Scots at Dunbar, swept north, seized the great castles and took from Scone Palace the Sacred Stone of Destiny on which all Scottish monarchs had been crowned. Edward had earned his title 'Hammer of the Scots'.

WILLIAM WALLACE

After a comparatively peaceful interlude, England's insidious interference provoked a serious backlash in 1297. William Wallace, a violent youth from Elderslie, became an outlaw after a scuffle with English soldiers in which a girl (some think she was his wife) who helped him escape was killed herself by the Sheriff of Lanark. Wallace returned to kill the sheriff, but didn't stop there; soon he had raised enough of an army to drive back the English, making him, for some months, master of southern Scotland. But Wallace wasn't supported by the nobles, who considered him low-born and, after being defeated at Falkirk by England's Edward I, he was hanged, drawn and quartered. His quarters were sent to Newcastle, Berwick, Stirling and Perth.

Scotland seemed crushed. However, one man, William Wallace, rose up and led a revolt, soundly defeating the English at Stirling Bridge. Edward responded by routing Wallace at Falkirk. In 1305, Wallace was captured, taken to London and brutally executed.

Robert the Bruce then took up the cause. After he was crowned king at Scone in 1306, he was forced to flee to Ireland. The story goes that when he was most discouraged, he watched a spider spinning a web and, inspired by this example of perseverance and courage, he resolved never to give up hope. The next year he returned to Scotland and captured Perth and Edinburgh. In 1314 at Bannockburn, he faced an army that outnumbered his forces three to one and had superior weapons.

However, Bruce had chosen his ground and his strategy skilfully and won a decisive victory. Bruce continued to hammer away at the English until 1328, when Edward III signed a treaty recognising the independence of Scotland. Robert the Bruce died the

Flodden Wall

Following the Battle of Flodden, the residents of Edinburgh hastily built the Flodden Wall to protect the city from sacking. A section of the wall still survives in the Vennel (alley) just off the Grassmarket.

following year, honoured as Scotland's saviour.

THE STEWARTS

In 1371 the reign of the Stewart, or Stuart, dynasty began. While the family was intelligent and talented, it seemed also prone to tragedy. The first three kings all came to power while still children; James I, II and III all died relatively young in tragic circumstances. James IV, who ruled 1488–1513, was an able king who quashed the rebellious Macdonald clan chiefs who had been styling themselves 'Lords of the Isles' since the mid-fourteenth century. In 1513 there was disaster: to honour the 'auld alliance' with France, James led his Scottish troops in an invasion over the English border. In the Battle of Flodden that followed, the Scots were crushed by the English in their worst ever defeat. Around 10,000 lost their lives, including the king himself and most of the peerage.

One result of the battle was to bring infant James V to the throne. His French second wife, Mary of Guise-Lorraine was the mother of Mary, Queen of Scots. James died prematurely in 1542, six days after his wife had given birth to his heir.

MARY, QUEEN OF SCOTS

The tragic events of this queen's life have captivated the imagination of generations. After the infant Mary was crowned, Henry VIII tried to force the betrothal of Mary to his son, Edward and thus unite the two crowns. At the age of five Mary was sent to France for safekeeping. Her pro-Catholic mother, supported by

French forces, took over as regent, a move that was not popular with most Scots.

At the age of fifteen, Mary was married to the heir to the French throne. He died soon after becoming king, however, and in 1561 Mary, a devout young Catholic widow, returned to Scotland to assume her throne. There she found the Protestant Reformation in full swing, led by John Knox. A follower of Geneva Protestant John Calvin, Knox was a bitter enemy of both the Roman Catholic and the Anglican Church. Mary's agenda was bound to cause trouble: to restore Roman Catholicism and to rule as queen of Scotland in the French style. The Scottish monarchs had been kings of the Scots, not of Scotland so they were answerable to the people – a fundamental difference. She alienated the lords who held the real power and came into conflict with Knox, who heaped insults on her in public.

Mary spent just six turbulent years as Scotland's queen. Scandals surrounded her. In 1565 she married Henry, Lord Darnley and the next year bore a son, the future James VI. Darnley was implicated in the murder of Mary's confidential secretary at Holyroodhouse. Darnley himself was murdered two years later and many suspected Mary's involvement. Doubts crystallised when, a few months later, she married one of the plot's ringleaders, the Earl of Bothwell.

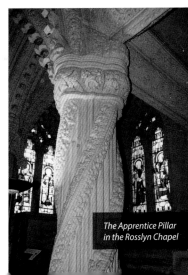

The Apprentice Pillar in the Rosslyn Chapel

Deposed and held captive, she made a daring escape to England, there to become a thorn in the side of her cousin, Elizabeth I and a rallying point for Catholic dissidents. Mary was kept in captivity in England for nearly twenty years until, in 1587, she was beheaded.

TOWARDS UNION WITH ENGLAND

After his mother's death, James VI assumed the throne as Scotland's first Protestant king. When Elizabeth died in 1603, James rode south to claim the English throne as James I. But the Union of Crowns did not bring instant harmony. The seventeenth century witnessed fierce religious and political struggles in Scotland. James and his son Charles I (1625–49) had to face opposition from Scottish churchmen. In 1638 Scots signed the National Covenant, giving them the right to their own form of Presbyterian worship.

Mary, Queen of Scots

When the civil war broke out in England, the Covenanters at first backed Parliament against Charles. After he was beheaded in 1649, the Scots backed Charles II. However, Presbyterianism was not formally established as the Church of Scotland until Catholic James VII (James II of England) was deposed in the Glorious Revolution of 1688, which brought Protestant joint monarchs, William III and Mary II of Orange to the English throne (1689–1702). In 1707, despite widespread Scottish opposition, England and Scotland signed the Act of Union. The Scots were to have minority representation in the upper and lower houses at Westminster, they were to keep their own courts and legal system and the status of the national Presbyterian Church was guaranteed. But Scottish nationalism was not so easily subdued.

THE JACOBITES

Four times in the next forty years the Jacobites tried to restore the exiled royal family to the throne. The most serious effort was the Rising Stewart, known as 'Bonnie Prince Charlie'. This grandson of James VII was 24 years old when he sailed from France disguised as a divinity student to land in Scotland in July 1745. Within two months he had rallied enough clan support to occupy Perth and Edinburgh. In early November he invaded England, pushing to Derby by 4 December.

However, English Jacobites failed to come to the aid of the rebellion and again, no help appeared from France. Charles' troops were hopelessly outnumbered. Reluctantly he agreed to retreat north and, by 20 December, they were back in Scotland. From this time on, the Jacobite cause went downhill. The final blow came at the Battle of Culloden Moor which was fought near Inverness on 16 April 1746. The weary Highlanders were subjected to a crushing defeat at the hands of superior government forces under the Duke of Cumberland.

In less than an hour, about 1200 of Charles's men were killed; many others, wounded and captured, were treated in a brutal manner that earned Cumberland the lasting sobriquet of 'Butcher'. Charles escaped, aided by Flora MacDonald, who became Scotland's romantic heroine. After spending five months as a fugitive in the Highlands and Western Isles, he left his country for good aboard a French ship.

THE AFTERMATH

Although the Jacobite cause was finished, Highlanders had to face harsh consequences. The clan structure was destroyed, Gaelic suppressed and wearing of the kilt or plaid was banned. Clans who had supported the rebellion lost their lands. Thousands of crofters (farmers of smallholdings) had to abandon their homes to wealthy sheep farmers from the south under the Highland Clearances programme. Many emigrated to the United States and Canada. Today the Highland glens still remain empty.

While the Highlands were emptying, the less troubled part of Scotland was booming. Glasgow's tobacco monopoly enriched its merchants and James Watt's invention of the steam engine made the Industrial Revolution possible. Glasgow, with its famous shipbuilding industry, became the 'Workshop of the Empire'.

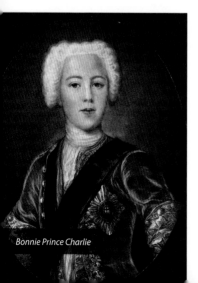

Bonnie Prince Charlie

Edinburgh began development into an international intellectual and cultural centre. The so-called 'Scottish Enlightenment' produced philosophers like David Hume and poets like Robert Burns.

Unlike England, with its rigid class system, Scotland's more democratic attitude made it far easier for poor boys to gain a university education. The work of Scottish scientists, writers, explorers, engineers and industrialists became famous worldwide. In the

1860s Queen Victoria and Prince Albert discovered the Highlands and made tartan apparel fashionable by adopting it themselves.

Yet with the political centre in Westminster and a system in place that gave precedence to English affairs, Scotland was never an equal partner in the union with England. During the privations of the Great Depression and the industrial downturn after World War II, Scots felt impotent and apathetic. But when North Sea oil was discovered, the failing Scottish economy did a turnaround, and with the new prosperity came a resurgence of Scottish national spirit.

Stewart standard

Bonnie Prince Charlie arrived at Glenfinnan on 19 August 1745 and raised the Stewart standard. He rallied 1200 clansmen ready to battle for the British throne. Seventy years later, Alexander MacDonald of Glenaladale built the Glenfinnan Memorial in memory of all the clansmen who had fought for the cause.

MODERN SCOTLAND

In 1997 the Scots voted overwhelmingly for the re-establishment of a Scottish Parliament. The new Scottish Parliament, which opened in 1999, gained control over all local affairs, such as education, economic development, agriculture and the environment, but with a limited ability to collect and control tax revenues. Nonetheless, many Scots saw this as a new beginning, a chance to assert their national identity and protect their culture and heritage. A state-of-the-art new Scottish Parliament building – way over budget and well past its original completion deadline – opened for business at Holyrood in 2004.

In the 2007 Scottish election, the Scottish National Party (SNP) gained power by a one-seat majority with its leader, Alex Salmond,

Bonnie Prince Charlie raised the Stewart standard at Glenfinnan

firmly installed as First Minister of the country. Over the next few years, Salmond pushed Westminster for further devolution, culminating in a 2014 referendum when the Scots voted to stay within the United Kingdom, with 55 percent in favour of the notion. The SNP had a remarkable landslide victory at the May 2015 general election, returning 56 out of 59 Scottish seats under the leadership of Nicola Sturgeon, although they lost 21 of these in the 2017 election. The 2016 Brexit referendum revealed further cracks in the UK: 52 percent of UK voters opted to leave the European Union (EU), while in Scotland, 62 percent voted to remain, prompting many SNP members to call for another independence referendum. However, Sturgeon's surprise resignation in 2023 – with Hamza Yusuf stepping up as the new First Minister – put the independence debate on the backburner.

Meanwhile, in the 2019 election, the SNP came storming back, securing 48 of the 59 available seats in Parliament.

HISTORICAL LANDMARKS

c. 6000 BC First signs of human settlement in Scotland.

AD 84 Romans beat the 'Caledonians' in the Battle of Mons Graupius.

AD 185 Romans withdraw behind the line marked by Hadrian's Wall.

5th century Gaelic-speaking 'Scots' enter the country from Ireland.

563 St Columba spreads Christianity in Scotland.

775–800 Norse forces occupy Hebrides, Orkney and Shetland.

843 Kenneth MacAlpin becomes the first King of the Scots.

1290 A succession crisis allows Edward I of England to seize control.

1297 William Wallace leads a revolt.

1305 Wallace taken to London and executed.

1306–28 Robert the Bruce wins independence back for Scotland.

1371 Reign of the Stewart dynasty begins.

1513 Defeat to the English in the Battle of Flodden, King James IV killed.

1542 Mary, Queen of Scots crowned at just six days old.

1561 Mary returns to Scotland from France to assume her throne.

1568 Mary flees to England, where she is imprisoned.

1603 James VI, Mary's son, unites the thrones as James I of England.

1638 National Covenant signed, starting a long period of rebellion.

1707 Act of Union between England and Scotland.

1745 'Bonnie Prince Charlie' takes back Scotland and invades England.

1750–1800 'Scottish Enlightenment'.

1765 James Watt invents the steam engine.

1780 Crofters lose their land in the Highland Clearances programme.

1997 Referendum votes in favour of separate Scottish Parliament.

2014 Scotland votes to stay within the United Kingdom.

2015 Landslide victory for the SNP in the election under Nicola Sturgeon.

2016 Scotland votes in favour of staying in the EU by 62 to 38 percent.

2017 SNP wins 35 seats in the general election, a loss of 21 seats from the previous 56 held.

2018 Glasgow School of Art devastated by second fire in four years.

2019 The SNP secures 48 of the 59 seats available in general election.

2023 Nicola Sturgeon resigns as First Minister, replaced by Hamza Yusuf.

Statue of Greyfriars Bobby
on Candlemaker Row

OUT AND ABOUT

Scotland's spectacular and varied scenery and rich historical heritage make it a fascinating country to explore. The country is about 565km (350 miles) from north to south and stretches in some parts as wide as 258km (160 miles), not counting the many islands of the Inner and Outer Hebrides. It is best to concentrate on a few areas, unless your time is unlimited. Scotland has a good network of roads in the Border country and motorways connecting major cities; however, the many winding roads in central Scotland and the single-lane roads in the Highlands can be slow going (see page 119). It's easy to explore Scotland via its excellent bus system (see page 132) or on one of the many tours to places of interest (see page 123).

In a country so rich in sights and experiences, only a selection can be presented below, but you'll find worthwhile sights, unspoiled villages and spectacular scenery wherever you go, as well as plenty of chances for outdoor sports and adventure.

EDINBURGH

The ancient, proud capital of Scotland is, of course, at its most lively during the Edinburgh Festival in August, but all year round it provides many sights and entertainments to enjoy – particularly when the sun is shining. Both the Old Town up against the rock of Edinburgh Castle and the New Town across the way are full of impressive architecture. And you'll find a remarkably congenial atmosphere – an unexpected bonus in a city of just over half a million people.

The seven hills of **Edinburgh ❶** look northward over the great Firth of Forth estuary or southward to gentle green countryside

Edinburgh's elegant rooftops

that rises into hills. Tour guides boast that Edinburgh is probably over 1500 years old and certainly it has been the capital of Scotland since 1437.

Despite all the echoes of the past, the city today seems decidedly young and vibrant. Most of the city's principal sights are within easy walking distance of each other or can be reached by public bus.

EDINBURGH CASTLE

Edinburgh's landmark and Scotland's most popular tourist attraction stands on an extinct volcano, high above the city. It is not known exactly how long ago the history of this great rock began, but there is archaeological evidence that there was human habitation here as early as the ninth century BC. A stone fortification was definitely erected late in the sixth century AD and the first proper castle was built in the eleventh century.

The entrance to **Edinburgh Castle A** (www.edinburghcastle. scot; charge) lies just beyond the Esplanade, which was once a site for the execution of witches, later a parade ground, and is now host to the famous **Military Tattoo**, performed during the annual **Edinburgh International Festival**.

The black naval cannons poking through the ramparts inside the gate have never been fired, but you'll see the cannon that booms out over the city every day (except Sunday) at one o'clock.

Tiny **St Margaret's Chapel** is the oldest surviving building in the castle, and probably in Edinburgh. Said to have been built by David I in the early twelfth century in honour of his mother, it has survived assaults over the centuries that destroyed the other structures on Castle Rock. The chapel, which has been simply restored with a plain white interior, is kept decorated with flowers by Scotswomen named Margaret. Close by, in a niche overlooking the city, is the Cemetery for Soldiers' Dogs, with the tombs of regimental mascots.

Further up the hill in Palace Yard is the **Great Hall**, claiming the finest hammer-beam ceiling in Britain. Built in 1503, the oak

EDINBURGH MILITARY TATTOO

In 1950 the city established a Military Tattoo at the same time as the Festival. The event features a highly polished show of military marching, pageantry, mock battles and horsemanship, and pyrotechnics, accompanied by the sounds of pipe-and-drum bands from around the world. All this happens nightly (except Sunday) against the backdrop of the magnificently floodlit castle in an arena erected in the Esplanade.

Tickets, which sell out months in advance, can be bought from www.edintattoo.co.uk.

timbers are joined together without a single nail, screw or bolt. It is here that Scotland's Parliament met for a century. In the **State Apartments** is Queen Mary's Room, the very small chamber in which Mary, Queen of Scots gave birth to James VI (later James I of England).

The castle's greatest treasures – the crown, sceptre and sword of Scotland and the Stone of Destiny – are in the **Crown Room**, reached through a series of rooms with displays detailing Scottish history. The rooms are often extremely crowded; on a busy day, more than 10,000 viewers file through here to see the oldest royal regalia in Europe. The gold-and-pearl crown was first used for the coronation of Robert the Bruce in 1306. It was altered in 1540, and Charles II wore it for the last time in 1651. The sword and sceptre were given to James IV by popes Alexander VI and Julius II. The

The famous Military Tattoo

Stone of Destiny, on which Scottish monarchs were traditionally crowned, was only returned to Scotland from captivity in Westminster Abbey in 1996; it had been carried away from Scone in 1296 by English king Edward I, as a symbol of his conquest of Scotland (see page 16).

In the back vault of the French prisons is kept **Mons Meg**, a stout cannon that was forged in Mons (hence the name) in the fifteenth century. The 6.6-ton monster ingloriously blew up two hundred years later while firing a salute to the Duke of Albany and York.

THE ROYAL MILE

The Royal Mile runs along the ridge from Edinburgh Castle downhill to the royal Palace of Holyroodhouse. The **Old Town's** famous thoroughfare, its cobbles now mostly smoothed, is actually about 2km (1.2 miles) long (the Scottish mile was longer than the English). As it descends, the

The Royal Mile

Royal Mile takes five names: Castlehill, Lawnmarket, High Street, Canongate and Abbey Strand.

In medieval times, this was Edinburgh's main drag, and enclosed by the city walls, the town grew upwards. Edinburghers delight in recounting how residents of the high tenements and narrow 'wynds' (alleys) used to toss slops from windows after a perfunctory shout of 'Gardyloo!' (the equivalent of 'garde à l'eau'). Today, it is lined with historic buildings, tourist shops, restaurants and pubs.

On Castlehill the **Camera Obscura** at the top of the **Outlook Tower** (www.camera-obscura.co.uk; charge) offers a fascinating fifteen-minute show via a periscope that reflects live images of prominent buildings and folk walking on the streets below; make sure to go when the weather is dry. Here, too, is **World of Illusions**, a labyrinth of family-friendly exhibits of optical illusions, holograms and clever visual trickery spread across five floors beneath the camera itself.

Opposite the tower, in the **Scotch Whisky Experience** (www. scotchwhiskyexperience.co.uk; charge), you will be transported (in a barrel) through the history of Scotland's 'water of life'.

Further along, in James Court, Dr Samuel Johnson once visited his biographer, James Boswell, a native of Edinburgh. In Brodie's Close the popular local story of Deacon Brodie is recalled: a respected city official and carpenter by day, he was a burglar by night (he made wax impressions of his clients' house keys). Finally arrested and condemned, he tried to escape death by wearing a steel collar under his shirt. Unfortunately for him, the gallows, which he himself had designed, worked perfectly. His double life inspired fellow Scot Robert Louis Stevenson to write *Dr Jekyll and Mr Hyde*.

The Royal Mile's best surviving example of a typical seventeenth-century tenement is **Gladstone's Land** (477B Lawnmarket; www.nts.org.uk; charge), which has been furnished in its original style, with a reconstructed shop booth on the ground floor; it would have once been home to various families living in extremely cramped conditions.

A brief detour down George IV Bridge takes you to the statuette of **Greyfriars Bobby**, a Skye terrier that allegedly waited by his master's grave in nearby Greyfriars Churchyard for fourteen years until dying of old age in 1872. Admiring the dog's loyalty, the authorities made Bobby a freeman of the city.

Across the road in Chambers Street stands the **National Museum of Scotland** Ⓑ (www.nms.ac.uk; free, charge for special exhibitions), resplendent following the restoration of the old Royal Museum building. The National Museum pays homage to Scotland and its history, as well as ethnography, archaeology, technology and the decorative arts. Highlights include the famous **Lewis chessmen**, idiosyncratic twelfth-century pieces carved from walrus ivory, along with pieces relating to the more significant periods

The impressive interior of the
National Museum of Scotland

of Scotland's past, including the Highland uprisings under Bonnie
Prince Charlie (whose silver travelling canteen is on display).

Back along the Royal Mile, **St Giles Cathedral** ⊙ (www.st
gilescathedral.org.uk; free, donations accepted), the High Kirk
of Scotland, dominates Parliament Square. Its famous tower spire
was built in 1495 as a replica of the Scottish crown. The oldest
elements of St Giles are the huge twelfth-century pillars that support the spire, but there was probably a church on the site since
854. John Knox preached here and is thought to be buried in the
rear graveyard. The soaring Norman interior of St Giles is filled
with memorials recalling the great moments of Scottish history,
while stained glass in the church dates from 1883 up to modern
times. Most beautiful is the **Thistle Chapel**: dating from 1911,
it is ornately carved out of Scottish oak; you'll see a stall for the
queen and princely seats for the sixteen Knights of the Thistle,
Scotland's oldest order of chivalry.

Across the street lie the **City Chambers**, designed by John Adam in the 1750s. Beneath them is Mary King's Close, one of the areas where, until the eighteenth century, people lived in crowded, unsanitary conditions that aided the spread of plague and disease.

Further down, **John Knox House D** (45 High Street; charge), dating from 1450, is the oldest surviving medieval building on the Royal Mile. Not only does it contain an excellent exhibit on the life of John Knox (1513–72), leader of the Scottish Reformation and one of the most important figures in Scottish history (see page 19), but it's also home to the **Scottish Storytelling Centre** (www.scottishstorytellingcentre.com; charge for events), which stages regular performances and events.

Across the High Street is the **Museum of Childhood** (www.edinburghmuseums.org.uk; free, charge for special exhibitions), with a display of children's toys and games through the centuries. At Canongate Tolbooth, the **People's Story** (www.edinburgh-museums.org.uk/venue/peoples-story-museum) is a social history museum, telling the stories of Edinburgh's ordinary people through reconstructions that capture the sounds, sights and smells of the past. Across the road is the **Museum of Edinburgh** (www.edinburghmuseums.org.uk/venue/museum-edinburgh), presenting local history exhibits from prehistoric times to the present.

The royal **Palace of Holyroodhouse E** (www.rct.uk; charge), at the end of the Royal Mile, began life in about 1500 as a mere guest house for the adjacent, now-ruined abbey. Much expanded and rebuilt in the seventeenth century, it has hosted numerous visiting monarchs (see page 19).

The long Picture Gallery showcases many portraits, purportedly of Scottish kings, which were dashed off between 1684–6 by Jacob de Wit the Younger, a Dutchman. In King James' Tower, up a winding inner stairway, are the apartments of Darnley and Mary, Queen of Scots. A plaque marks the spot where the Rizzio, Mary's Italian

Inside the state-of-the-art Scottish Parliament at Holyrood

secretary, was stabbed with a dagger more than 56 times before the queen's eyes.

Above Holyroodhouse looms **Arthur's Seat** Ⓕ, which can be climbed via Holyrood Park. Back on Holyrood Road, you'll see the **Scottish Parliament building** Ⓖ (www.parliament.scot/visit; free), a magnificent showpiece designed by the Catalan architect Enric Miralles. Nearby, also on Holyrood Road, is **Our Dynamic Earth** (www.dynamicearth.co.uk; charge), a permanent exhibition with displays on the formation and evolution of the planet.

NEW TOWN

Until late in the eighteenth century, Edinburgh was confined to the crowded, unhealthy Old Town, along the ridge from the castle or in the wynds beneath the Royal Mile. The population, which numbered about 25,000 in 1700, had nearly tripled by 1767, when James Craig won a planning competition for an extension

The Scott Monument

to the city. With significant help from the noted Robert Adam, he created the **New Town**, a complete complex of Georgian architecture.

At the centre of the New Town is Edinburgh's main artery, bustling **Princes Street**, which had developed into Edinburgh's principal thoroughfare by the middle of the nineteenth century, a role it has retained ever since. **Princes Street Gardens**, the city's green centrepiece, replaced what was once a fetid stretch of water called Nor' Loch. Rising from the gardens is the Gothic spire of the **Scott Monument** (www.edinburghmuseums.org.uk; charge), which was erected in 1844 and has a statue of Sir Walter with his dog and statuettes of Scott's literary characters at its base. Inside the memorial, a tightly winding spiral staircase climbs 287 steps to a narrow platform near the top, from where you can enjoy inspiring vistas of the city and beyond.

A sloping road known as the Mound passes through the gardens. Here, behind the Royal Scottish Academy, is the **Scottish National Gallery** Ⓗ (www.nationalgalleries.org; free, charge for special exhibitions), a small but distinguished collection. Look for Van Dyck's *Lomellini Family*, Rubens' *The Feast of Herod*, Velázquez's *Old Woman Cooking Eggs*, and Sir Edwin Landseer's famous *Monarch of the Glen*. The English school is represented by Reynolds, Turner and Gainsborough. Don't miss the many paintings by the city's own Henry Raeburn, especially his well-known work, the *Rev. Robert Walker Skating on Duddingston Loch*.

At the west end of Princes Street is **Charlotte Square**, the Neoclassical centrepiece of the New Town, designed in 1792 by Robert Adam, Scotland's most celebrated architect of the eighteenth century. The eleven houses on the north side of the square with their symmetrical facades are considered to be his finest work. At No. 7 Charlotte Square, **Georgian House** (www.nts.org. uk; charge) has been restored in period style by the National Trust for Scotland. In the dining room is a splendid table setting of Wedgwood and Sheffield silver cutlery, and in the bed-chamber a marvellous medicine chest as well as a nineteenth-century water closet called 'the receiver'.

The excellent **Scottish National Gallery of Modern Art** (www. nationalgalleries.org; free, charge for special exhibitions) is housed in two Neoclassical buildings, Modern One and Modern Two, set in parkland dotted with sculptures by important artists such as Henry Moore. The gallery space has an international collection as well as work by Scottish artists, and it also hosts touring exhibits.

Along Inverleith Row extends the thirty hectares (75 acres) of the much-admired **Royal Botanic Garden** (www.rbge.org.

National Gallery

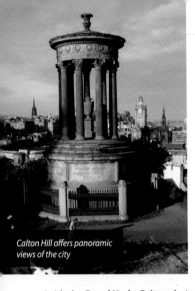

Calton Hill offers panoramic views of the city

uk; gardens free, charge for glasshouses) with a huge collection of rhododendrons and a remarkable rock garden, as well as cavernous plant houses.

At the east end of Princes Street is **Calton Hill**, reached via Waterloo Place. Here you'll find the old City Observatory that has been redeveloped as an arts centre, and from the top of the Nelson Monument there is a fine panoramic view.

On the waterfront at Leith the **Royal Yacht Britannia** (www.royalyachtbritannia.co.uk; charge) is docked. Launched in 1953, **Britannia** was used by the royal family for 44 years for state visits, diplomatic functions and royal holidays; you can roam around the yacht itself, which has been largely kept as she was while in service.

EXCURSIONS IN LOTHIAN

From Edinburgh you can take several excursions by bus to points of interest in the countryside. One of the shortest is to the huge **Hopetoun House** near South Queensferry, ten miles (16km) west of Edinburgh (www.hopetoun.co.uk; charge), a fine example of Neoclassical eighteenth-century architecture. The house has fine original furnishings as well as paintings by Dutch and Italian masters and is set in one hundred acres (41 hectares) of parkland with herds of red deer. Its gardens were designed in the grand style of Versailles.

Nearby at Linlithgow, overlooking the pewter waters of the loch, stand the ruins of **Linlithgow Palace** (www.historicenvironment. scot; charge), which was the birthplace of Mary, Queen of Scots in 1542. James V, Mary's father, gave the fountain in the courtyard to his wife Mary of Guise as a wedding present. The magnificent, galleried Great Hall measures 94ft (28m) in length, and enough of the enormous building still stands for the visitor to imagine what life must have been like here.

Situated alongside is the **Church of St Michael**, one of the best medieval parish churches in Britain and a fine example of the Scottish Decorated style, where a ghost is said to have warned James IV not to fight against England shortly before he and so many Scots were killed at the Battle of Flodden.

Golf courses, beaches, and pleasant villages make East Lothian a popular holiday destination. A pleasant coastal walk connects North Berwick and Gullane Bay, and at **Dirleton**, you will find a scattering of original stone cottages surrounding a large village green beneath a ruined castle. You can take a boat from North Berwick to glide around the bulbous Bass Rock, where you will glimpse some of the eight thousand gannets which easily outnumber the other feathered inhabitants such as puffins, shags, kittiwakes and cormorants.

Near Seacliff beach are the formidable reddish ruins of 600-year-old **Tantallon Castle** (www.historicenvironment.scot; charge) high up on a cliff. Queen Victoria visited this fortress of the Black

Forth Rail Bridge

About eight miles (13km) west of Edinburgh is one of the Victorian era's greatest engineering feats, the Forth Rail Bridge. Completed in 1890, the bridge comprises three huge cantilevers joined by two suspended spans, for a total length of 4746ft (1447m). For many years it was the world's longest bridge.

Douglas clan in 1898, and probably peered into the well, cut 89ft (27m) through sheer rock.

In the Pentland Hills, just south of Edinburgh, **Rosslyn Chapel** ❷ (www.rosslynchapel.com) in Roslin, Midlothian, is an unusual church. Built in 1446, it is richly decorated with carvings both pagan and Christian – biblical stories, 'green men', references to the Knights Templar, and plants of the New World that pre-date Columbus's voyage of discovery.

SOUTHERN SCOTLAND

The many ruined castles and abbeys bear silent witness to the turbulent history of the Borders and Galloway area – centuries of conflict between the Scots and the English and also between Scots and Scots. Today this is a region of peaceful countryside, packed with literary associations, with historic houses, tranquil rivers and attractive market towns.

THE APPRENTICE

Contained within the small, fifteenth-century Rosslyn Chapel is the most elaborate stone carving in Scotland. The Seven Deadly Sins, the Seven Cardinal Virtues and a dance of death are extravagantly represented in bas-relief, although interest tends to focus on the Apprentice Pillar with its intricate and abundant flowers and foliage. The story has never been authenticated, but the pillar is said to have been carved by an apprentice while his master was away. The work was so fine that the master, on his return, flew into a jealous rage and killed the apprentice. Three carved heads at the end of the nave are alleged to depict the unfortunate youth, his grieving mother and his master.

THE BORDERS

Rolling green hills, woods and farmland run from Lothian into Scotland's Borders region. The hilly countryside around **Peebles** ❸ is worth exploring, particularly the beautiful Manor Valley. Nearby there are two quite outstanding gardens: **Kailzie Gardens** (on B7062 southeast of Peebles; www.kailziegardens.com; charge) and **Dawyck Botanic Gardens** (on B712 southwest; www.rbge.org.uk; charge).

To the east along the River Tweed, near Innerleithen, is **Traquair House** (www.traquair.co.uk; charge), dating back some 1000 years and the oldest inhabited house in Scotland. In all, 27 Scottish and English kings have stayed here. It also sheltered Catholic priests and supporters of the Jacobite cause, and is full of curiosities like a secret stairway to a priest's room and a fourteenth-century hand-printed bible. **Abbotsford House** (www.scottsabbotsford.com; charge), further down the Tweed, past Galashiels, was the home of **Sir Walter Scott**, who spent the last twenty years of his life here, writing frantically in an effort to pay his debts. Visitors may inspect six rooms containing his personal belongings, including his small writing desk, and collection of arms and armour.

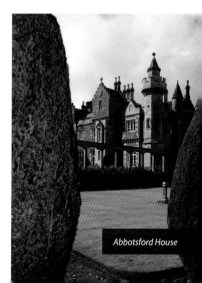
Abbotsford House

THE BORDER ABBEYS

The **Border abbeys** were all founded in the twelfth

Melrose Abbey

The destruction caused by Edward II's attack on Melrose Abbey in 1322 prompted Robert the Bruce to fund the abbey's restoration. His heart is said to be buried near the abbey's high altar, but subsequent excavations have failed to locate any trace of it.

century during the reign of David I, four great southern monasteries that stand in varying degrees of ruin today.

Always vulnerable to invading forces from England, the abbeys endured frequent sacking, restoration, then new destruction, again and again. The impressive remnants of **Melrose Abbey** (www.historicenvironment. scot; charge), built of rose-coloured stone, are set off by close-trimmed lawns. The site is dominated by the abbey church, which has lost its west front, and whose nave is reduced to the elegant window arches and chapels of the south aisle. You will also find a small visitor centre and a museum crowded with relics opposite the entrance.

Kelso Abbey (www.historicenvironment.scot; free) was founded in 1128 and took 84 years to complete. Just one arcaded transept tower and a facade are all that remain to suggest the original dimensions of the oldest and once the richest southern Scottish monastery.

Closer to the English border on the River Tweed, **Jedburgh Abbey ❹** (www.historicenvironment.scot; charge) is a more complete structure. The main aisle of the church, which is lined by a three-tiered series of nine arches, is nearly intact.

Entry is through the visitor centre at the bottom of the hill, where you can view Jedburgh's most treasured archeological find, the Jedburgh Comb, carved around 1100 from walrus ivory and decorated with a griffin and a dragon. Also in Jedburgh is **Mary, Queen of Scots' Visitor Centre** (www.liveborders.org.uk; free), a rather cursory insight into Mary's complex life through its assortment of paintings, textiles and associated objects, including Mary's own death mask.

Dryburgh Abbey (www.historicenvironment.scot; charge) is probably the most beautiful of the four abbeys, and sits among stately beeches and cedars on the banks of the River Tweed. Some of the monks' cloister survives, but little now remains of the church; here, too, is the grave of Sir Walter Scott.

From Bemersyde Hill, which is reached from Dryburgh via Gattonside along a beautiful tree-tunnelled road (B6356), you can enjoy **Scott's View**, a panorama of the three peaks of the Eildon Hills and the writer Sir Walter Scott's favourite scenic spot.

AYRSHIRE, DUMFRIES AND GALLOWAY

Ayrshire is **Burns Country**, so called after Robert Burns, the national poet of Scotland who was born in 1759 in Alloway, just south of the thriving coastal town of Ayr, and lived in this area most of his life. Here are all the echoes of his narrative poem 'Tam o'Shanter' and the 'Auld Brig o' Doon' which has spanned the River Doon in Alloway for seven hundred years. Burns' liking for his wee dram and bonnie lassies seems to have enhanced his already monumental reputation.

Dryburgh Abbey ruins

Burns National Heritage Park

In Alloway you can visit the **Robert Burns Birthplace Museum** ❺ (www.nts.org.uk; charge), home to a voluminous and illuminating exhibition including books and letters, his parlour chair and desk, and the pistol he used as an exciseman. Close by is his carefully preserved birthplace, **Burns Cottage**, a low, whitewashed, single-room thatched cottage where animals and people lived under the same roof; you'll also see the box bed where Burns and three of his brothers used to sleep as children; even his razor and shaving mirror are displayed.

You can follow the **Burns Heritage Trail** down to Dumfries where he died in 1796. Inside **Burns' House** (www.dgculture.co.uk/venue/robert-burns-house; free), one of the bedroom windows bears his signature, scratched with his diamond ring; the poet is buried in a mausoleum in nearby St Michael's Churchyard.

It is well worth making a swift detour to visit seventeenth-century **Drumlanrig Castle** (www.drumlanrigcastle.co.uk; charge) near Thornhill. Of all the priceless treasures sheltered within this pink sandstone mansion, you'll likely linger longest over Rembrandt's *Old Woman Reading* on the main stairway; there are also paintings by Holbein and Gainsborough. Napoleon's dispatch box is also here, a gift from Wellington to the owner of the castle, as well as a handful of relics belonging to Bonnie Prince Charlie (see page 21).

South of Dumfries you will find the lovely red sandstone ruins of **Sweetheart Abbey** (www.historicenvironment.scot; charge), which was founded in the thirteenth century by the pious (and rich) Devorgilla Balliol, Lady of Galloway. She dedicated it to her husband, John Balliol, who died at a young age and whose embalmed heart she carried around with her in a silver box until her own death in 1289.

Also south of Dumfries, do not miss the moated fairytale **Caerlaverock Castle** (www.historicenvironment.scot; charge), a picture-perfect thirteenth-century ruined castle built from rich local red sandstone, triangular in layout and with a mighty double-towered gatehouse.

On the other side of the River Nith, **Ruthwell Cross**, named after its hamlet, is kept in a pretty church surrounded by weathered

The Brig o' Doon features in Burns' poetry

Gretna Green

Just over the border from England is the small town of Gretna Green, which became celebrated for celebrating marriages. It was the first available community where eloping couples from England could take advantage of Scotland's different marriage laws. Many a makeshift wedding ceremony was performed at the Old Blacksmith's, now converted into a visitor centre, and many couples still choose to be married at Gretna Green today.

tombstones. Standing 18ft (5.5m) high and covered with sculpted figures and runic inscriptions, this great monument was carved out of brownish-pink stone some 1300 years ago. If the church is locked, the key can be found in a box at the manse next door.

Not only does southwest Scotland have beautiful shorelines, unspoiled moors and forest scenery, it also claims milder weather than any other part of the country. Just north of Newton Stewart is **Galloway Forest Park**, where you can walk through wild hill country. To the extreme southwest is the peninsula called the Rhinns of Galloway.

The **Logan Botanic Garden** (www.rbge.org.uk; charge) is home to Scotland's finest collection of tree ferns and, among many palms and other warm-weather species, superb magnolias from western China.

South of the gardens is the most southerly point in Scotland, the high-cliffed Mull of Galloway, where you can see the Isle of Man on a clear day.

On a pastoral hill midway up the peninsula is a stone chapel which contains several of Scotland's oldest Christian relics: the **Kirkmadrine Stones**, which consist of three stones and various fragments dating back to the fifth century.

CULZEAN CASTLE

One of Scotland's top attractions, **Culzean Castle** ❻ (www.nts.org.uk; charge) towers above the sea on a rugged stretch of the Ayrshire coast. It stands in an estate of over five hundred acres (202 hectares) of parkland and stately formal gardens. Now a National Trust property, the castle dates mostly from the late eighteenth century when it was transformed for the Kennedy family from a sixteenth-century tower house by the architect Robert Adam. The oval staircase is considered one of Adam's finest designs; the best room is the circular drawing room with its ceiling in three pastel shades, a perfect example of Scottish Enlightenment, its windows overlooking the waves of the Firth of Clyde breaking on the rocks 151ft (46m) below. The grounds have much to offer, from the Fountain Court with its orangery and terraces to the walled

Culzean Castle

Glen Rosa, Arran

garden with a stone grotto and fruit-filled greenhouses and the quirky follies dotted around the estate. Waymarked trails ramble through a huge deer park filled with deer and llamas, past woodland children's playgrounds to soaring cliffs and shingle beaches.

ARRAN

The unspoilt **Isle of Arran** ❼ in the Firth of Clyde has been called 'Scotland in miniature'. Car ferries ply regularly between Arran's capital, Brodick, and Ardrossan on the Ayrshire coast, while a smaller ferry links Lochranza in the north to Claonaig in Kintyre. Brodick village nestles on a bay in the shadow of **Goatfell**, which, at 2867ft (874m), is the highest peak on Arran. On Brodick Bay, **Brodick Castle** (www.nts.org.uk; charge) contains a wealth of treasures, but more impressive is its extensive **country park** filled with exotic plants and trees.

Red deer roam the island's beautiful mountain glens and can often be seen in North Glen Sannox between Lochranza and Sannox. Arran is above all an island for hill walkers or climbers; the most dramatic scenery is in the north of the island, where there are ten summits over 2000ft (610m) and dozens of ridge routes. In the south the topography is gentler, with pleasant hills around the villages of Lamlash and Whiting Bay.

Among the hundred or so species of birds known to frequent Arran are peregrine falcons and rare golden eagles. Seals claim the rocks along Arran's 56 miles (90km) of coast and basking sharks can be seen offshore in the summer. Arran has some outstanding archaeological sites. There are Neolithic chamber tombs, such as the one at **Torrylinn**, near Lagg, and Bronze Age stone circles around Machrie on the west coast. Towards the island's southwest corner on a wild, cliff-backed coast are the **King's Caves**, where Robert the Bruce is said to have taken refuge in 1307. The caves are a twenty-minute walk from the car park.

GLASGOW

Glasgow ❽ has undergone major changes during the twenty-first century, and has not only cleaned its splendid Victorian buildings and generally polished up its act, but now proudly presents itself

The 1996-built House for an Art Lover

as one of Europe's major centres for culture and the arts. The city is home to the Scottish Opera, Scottish Ballet, the Royal Scottish National Orchestra and the BBC Scottish Symphony Orchestra, and stages several superb festivals including Celtic Connections in January and TRNSMT in July.

At the heart of Glasgow lies **George Square**, overlooked by the impressive **City Chambers** (www.glasgow.gov.uk; free, guided tours only), opened by Queen Victoria in 1888; a statue of her on horseback is on the west side of the square. Elsewhere, there are other assorted luminaries such as James Watt and wee Robbie Burns. Glasgow's sophisticated main shopping area is the Buchanan Quarter, which is a block northwest of George Square.

THE GLASGOW BOYS

The late nineteenth and early twentieth centuries were a time of artistic ferment in Glasgow, but because of the hide-bound local arts establishment, Glasgow artists often had to look for recognition outside Scotland. Charles Rennie Mackintosh was a leading figure in the Art Nouveau movement on the continent, and influenced designers such as Frank Lloyd Wright as far afield as Chicago, but was not admired at home.

Others who suffered the same fate were painters Sir James Guthrie, Robert MacGregor, William Kennedy, Sir John Lavery and Edward Arthur Walton. After a successful London exhibition, the 'Glasgow School' was born, but the artists always called themselves the 'Glasgow Boys'. More recently, a new generation of Glasgow Boys began to emerge from the School of Art in the 1970s and 1980s. The works of Glasgow Boys of both generations can be seen in the Kelvingrove Art Gallery and the Gallery of Modern Art (GoMA; www.glasgowlife.org.uk/museums; free).

TRACES OF MACKINTOSH

The city is closely connected with Scottish architect **Charles Rennie Mackintosh**. Almost forgotten by his native city at the time of his death, he has become world famous, and today his unique vision is a prominent feature of Glasgow's art scene. His most famous work is the **Glasgow School of Art** (www.gsa.ac.uk; free), which was seriously damaged

Burrell Collection

by fire in 2014 and, while undergoing restoration, sadly suffered another devastating fire in 2018.

While the school is being restored, the neighbouring Reid building, housing the visitor centre, shop and exhibitions spaces, also remains closed and tours are cancelled until further notice (check website for updates).

Opened in 1996, the **House for an Art Lover** (Bellahouston Park; www.houseforanartlover.co.uk; charge) was created from a portfolio Mackintosh submitted for a design competition in 1901, following a brief to 'design a house in a thoroughly modern style, where one can be lavishly entertained'.

The evocative rooms of Mackintosh's own house have been preserved next to the **Hunterian Art Gallery** Ⓐ at Glasgow University (www.gla.ac.uk/hunterian; free), which itself has some wonderful works by James Whistler and William McTaggart. Elsewhere, stop off at No. 97 Buchanan Street for the **Willow Tea Rooms** (www.

willowtearooms.co.uk), a survivor of a series of tearooms inspired by the architect. For more information on Mackintosh attractions in the city contact the Charles Rennie Mackintosh Society (www.crmsociety.com).

MAJOR MUSEUMS

Glasgow's most important museum is the **Burrell Collection B** (2060 Pollokshaws Road; www.burrellcollection.com; free, charge for special exhibitions) in Pollok Country Park to the southwest of the city centre. Opened in 1983, it holds the thousands of pieces amassed by shipping tycoon Sir William Burrell, including everything from ancient Greek statues to Impressionist paintings, medieval tapestries to stained glass. Also in the park is Pollok House and its fine collection of Spanish art.

In Kelvingrove Park is the city's splendid **Art Gallery and Museum** (Argyle Street; www.glasgowlife.org.uk/museums; free, charge for special exhibitions). On display are a collection of seventeenth-century Dutch paintings, including Rembrandt's masterpiece *A Man in Armour*, as well as some French Impressionists, nineteenth-century Scottish paintings and works by the Glasgow Boys. Other highlights include the Charles Rennie Mackintosh and Glasgow Style Gallery and a living bee exhibition.

Also giving a fascinating look into Glasgow's past is the **Tenement House** (www.nts.org.uk; charge). Miss Agnes Toward, who lived here from 1911 until 1965, never threw anything away, nor did she ever attempt to modernise the flat; the result is a wonderful insight into early twentieth-century social history.

OLD GLASGOW

Cathedral Street, northeast of the centre, brings you to the city's fine **Cathedral C** (www.glasgowcathedral.org.uk; free), the only medieval cathedral in Scotland that has survived intact. Parts of it are almost 800 years old, and it has an unusual two-level construction; the lower church contains the tomb of St Mungo (Kentigern), the city's patron saint. Above the church is the **Necropolis**, filled with the extravagant tombs of the city's late, great Victorians.

Across the street is **Provand's Lordship** 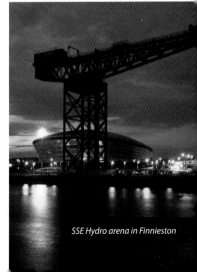 (www.glasgowlife.org.uk/museums; free), the oldest house in Glasgow. Originally, the fifteenth-century house was home to the cathedral administrative clergy; with its thick stone walls, it is a rare example of Scottish domestic architecture.

Opposite is the **St Mungo Museum of Religious Life and Art** (www.glasgowlife.org.uk/museums; free), comprising three galleries with a wealth of objects, notably a rare Kalabari Screen – an ancestral funerary screen from Nigeria featuring three wood-carved figures – and a fabulous bronze sculpture of a dancing Shiva, the Hindu god.

Head south down High Street to London Road to reach **Glasgow Green**, one of the city's many public parks – the oldest in Britain. Here, you can learn about the working life of Glaswegians throughout history in the **People's Palace** (www.glasgowlife.org.uk/museums; free). The nearby Barras indoor market, open weekends, will give you the chance to rub shoulders with local people and perhaps even pick up a bargain or two.

SSE Hydro arena in Finnieston

The Falkirk Wheel

THE WATERFRONT

More contemporary developments can be seen by the old docks to the west of the city centre. On the north bank of the Clyde is the **Scottish Event Campus**, which incorporates the OVO Hydro arena, the SEC Centre and the SEC Armadillo (this distinctive structure was designed by Sir Norman Foster).

Almost opposite, on the south bank, is the stunning titanium-clad **Glasgow Science Centre E** (www.glasgowsciencecentre.org; charge). This comprises three separate buildings: the Science Mall, which contains educational exhibits and a planetarium; the revolving 120ft (400m) Glasgow Tower with views as far as Ben Lomond; and an IMAX cinema.

To the west, beyond Stobcross Quay and adjacent to Glasgow Harbour, the futuristic interactive **Riverside Museum** (www.glasgowlife.org.uk/museums; free) is home to a huge, dramatically displayed collection of transport exhibits, including trains, boats, trams, bikes and cars. The Tall Ship, a three-masted Clyde-built barque from 1896, is moored nearby.

CENTRAL SCOTLAND

STIRLING

With its proud Renaissance castle commanding the major route between the Lowlands and the Highlands, **Stirling** ❾ for centuries saw much of Scotland's worst warfare. Guides at the castle regale visitors with tales of sieges, intrigue, dastardly murders and atrocities, and an audio-visual presentation just off the castle esplanade brings the savage saga vividly to life. In contrast to sober Edinburgh Castle, **Stirling Castle** (www.stirlingcastle.scot; charge) has a facade covered with all sorts of carvings. Most of the castle dates back about five hundred years, though the rock was fortified at least four centuries earlier. The **Palace** was built by James V in Renaissance style, and of interest here are the Stirling Heads, carved roundels that are possibly portraits of members

THE FALKIRK WHEEL

In 2002 Scotland re-asserted itself in the world of engineering by unveiling an iconic landmark, the Falkirk Wheel (www.scottishcanals.co.uk; charge). Named after the nearby town in central Scotland, the wheel is the world's only rotating boat lift. Built at a cost of over £17 million, the structure connects the Forth and Clyde Canal to the Union Canal, re-establishing the link between Edinburgh and Glasgow. Beneath the wheel, the **visitor centre** sells tickets for the **boat trip** from the lower basin into the wheel, along the Union Canal, and back again.

Stirling Castle is around 500 years old

of the court. Mary, Queen of Scots spent her early childhood here, and she was crowned as an infant in the **Chapel Royal**. The **Great Hall**, which faces the upper square, was once the greatest medieval chamber in Scotland, suitable for holding sessions of Parliament, but it later suffered through two centuries of use as a military barracks. Restoration has returned it to its original grandeur. Here, too, is the Museum of the Argyll and Sutherland Highlanders, containing banners, regimental silver, and artefacts that go back to the Battle of Waterloo. Fittingly, a statue of Robert the Bruce is on the Esplanade.

Nearby, the medieval **Church of the Holy Rude** (www. churchoftheholyrude.co.uk; charge), where the infant James VI was crowned in 1567, has a magnificent medieval hammerbeam oak roof.

Seven battlefields can be seen from the castle. In 1297, William Wallace defeated the English at Stirling Bridge. The **Wallace**

Monument is at Abbey Craig, east of the town centre, while the battlefield of **Bannockburn** is visible to the south of the castle. Here you'll find the **Battle of Bannockburn Experience** (www. nts.org.uk; charge), where the National Trust presents a 3D visual show bringing to life Robert the Bruce's epic victory over the English in 1314. Commemorating this triumph is an equestrian statue of **Robert the Bruce** with the inscription of his declaration: 'We fight not for glory nor for wealth nor for honour, but only and alone we fight for freedom, which no good man surrenders but with his life'.

Just north of Stirling, 700-year-old **Dunblane Cathedral** (www. historicenvironment.scot; free) is one of the finest examples of Gothic church architecture in Scotland. It is about a century older than **Doune Castle** (www.historicenvironment.scot; charge) just

Loch Lomond

to the west. A fortress-residence and once a Stuart stronghold, it is one of the best-preserved castles of its period. It has a central courtyard and Great Hall with an open-timbered roof and a minstrel's gallery.

LOCH LOMOND AND THE TROSSACHS

Romantically connected with the legend of Rob Roy, Scotland's folk hero, the **Trossachs** – which probably means 'bristly places', after the area's wooded crags – is a region of lovely lochs, glens and bens (mountain peaks), and craggy hills. Callander is a good centre from which to explore the Trossachs, with information available at the excellent tourist office on Mani Street. You can take a cruise on nearby **Loch Katrine**, the setting of Sir Walter Scott's poem *The Lady of the Lake*, on the Victorian steamer *Sir Walter Scott*, which leaves from Trossachs Pier. Salmon may well be leaping up the easily accessible Falls of Leny below Loch Lubnaig. Between Callander and Aberfoyle, the Duke's Pass has some fine views, and to the south is the **Queen Elizabeth Forest Park**, whose woodland walks offer a chance to spot wildlife.

Loch Lomond ❿, the largest freshwater expanse in Great Britain, runs about 24 miles (39km) north to south. Ben Lomond (3192ft/973m) and companion peaks look down on the sometimes choppy water at the north end of the loch, while to the south the landscape is tranquil and rolling. **Luss** is the prettiest of the little lochside villages, while the best reason to stop in **Balloch** is the **Loch Lomond Bird of Prey Centre** (www.lbopc.co.uk; charge), which keeps a fantastic display of owls, hawks, falcons and kestrels. A number of cruises set sail on Loch Lomond from Balloch, Tarbet, Inversnaid, Rowardennan and Luss. The West Highland Way provides a scenic footpath along the east bank of Loch Lomond.

To the west of Loch Lomond at the northern end of Loch Fyne, **Inveraray Castle** (www.inveraray-castle.com; charge), with its pointed turrets and Gothic design, contains a wealth of treasures. Home of the Dukes of Argyll, it has been the headquarters of Clan Campbell (called 'uncrowned kings of the Highlands') since the fifteenth century, although the present building dates only from between 1740 and 1790. The impressive interior holds a collection of Regency furniture; Chinese porcelain; portraits by Gainsborough, Ramsey and Raeburn; and an armoury with an amazing array of broadswords, Highland rifles, and medieval halberds. The guides point out with pride the portrait of the sixth duke, said both to have gambled away a fortune and to have fathered 398 illegitimate children.

Further south along Loch Fyne are the delightful **Crarae Garden** ⑪ (www.nts.org.uk; charge), with many unusual plants, such as the Himalayan rhododendrons, and plants from Tasmania and New

St Andrews' famous golf course

The RRS Discovery

Zealand. You can choose from several walks over the 50 acres (20 hectares) of hillside, all within earshot of a plunging brook.

FIFE

Dunfermline is dominated by the ruins of the **Abbey and Palace of Dunfermline** (www.historicenvironment.scot; free). King Malcolm Canmore made Dunfermline his capital around 1060, and his pious queen, St Margaret, founded the Benedictine abbey, though of the great abbey church, only the nave with its massive Norman arches survives.

Nearby, the fourteenth-century **Abbot House** has an interesting historical display. Industrialist and philanthropist Andrew Carnegie was born here, and his birthplace cottage and museum are open to visitors (www.carnegiebirthplace.com; free).

Also in this area is **Culross** (www.nts.org.uk), thought to be the birthplace of St Mungo, and now a wonderfully preserved seventeenth- and eighteenth-century village restored by the National Trust for Scotland. Among places of historic interest are Bruce's Palace from 1577 and the ruined abbey and Abbey House. The Trust runs guided tours (April–Oct) departing from the palace reception.

The most famous place on the Fife coast is **St Andrews** ⑫, where golf has been played for five hundred years. It's possible, if you are an experienced golfer, to tee off on the **Old Course** (see page 91), although there are several other courses for those less capable. Learn more about golf at the **R&A World Golf Museum** (www.worldgolfmuseum.co.uk; charge). This pleasant seaside resort is also home to Scotland's oldest university (founded in 1413), with buildings dotted all over town. Here also is the ruin of what was Scotland's largest-ever cathedral, an enormous structure built in the twelfth and thirteenth centuries, where the marriage of James V and Mary of Guise took place. For culture, the local theatre, The Byre, is well regarded.

The picturesque **East Neuk** fishing villages on Fife's southeastern coast are more dependent on tourism than fishing nowadays. **Crail** is a little port with a Dutch-style tolbooth (courthouse jail) and restored buildings: a photographer's delight. **Anstruther** (which the locals pronounce 'Anster'), once the herring capital of Scotland, is worth a stop for the Scottish Fisheries Museum (www. scotfishmuseum.org; charge) with its realistic fisherman's cottage of about 1900, magnificent ship models, whale tusks, and a display about trawlers.

From here you can take a boat trip to the **Isle of May**, a bird sanctuary with cliffs that climb to 249ft (76m).

Across the Firth of Tay, which is spanned by one of the world's longest railway bridges as well as a road bridge, lies **Dundee**, famous maritime and industrial centre. Docked in the harbour is the Royal Navy's oldest ship, HMS *Unicorn*, and Captain Scott's

Three Js

The industrial history of Dundee is often described by 'the three Js' – jute, jam and journalism. The city's rapid growth in population during the 19th century was due in large part to the jute industry, now completely gone. The only 'J' still thriving is journalism – newspaper and comic publisher D.C. Thomson & Co have been in business for over a century.

ship, the RRS *Discovery*, built here at the turn of the twentieth century and used in his polar expeditions. Pride of place, however, goes to the magnificent (www.vam. ac.uk/dundee; free, charge for special exhibitions) – the only other V&A museum in the world outside of London – whose galleries showcase hundreds of historically significant objects, such as Charles Macintosh's waterproof fabric and the pioneering work of Patrick Geddes in improving urban living.

PERTH AND SCONE PALACE

Perth ⓭ was Scotland's medieval capital, and has many reminders of its historic heritage. John Knox preached in the **Church of St John**, founded in 1126, inspiring his followers to destroy many monasteries in the area in 1559. Just two miles (3km) north of Perth, the pale red sandstone **Scone Palace** (www.scone-palace. co.uk; charge) was built on the site of one of these monasteries. From the ninth to the thirteenth century, Scone (pronounced 'Scoon') guarded the famous **Stone of Destiny**, on which the kings of the Scots were crowned. Edward I, believing in the symbolic magic of the stone, carried it away in 1296 and took it to London where, until 1996, it rested beneath the chair on which the English kings were crowned in Westminster Abbey. Romantics, however, believe that the stone, now on display in Edinburgh Castle (see page 30), is not the original, but a replica produced by the Scots

Glamis Castle

to fool Edward, and suggest that the real stone (which they think was covered with carvings) is still hidden in Scotland.

In the palace, the ancestral home of the Earls of Mansfield, are many treasures, including early Sèvres, Derby, and Meissen porcelain, and artefacts such as the embroideries of Mary, Queen of Scots. The Long Gallery shelters over eighty Vernis Martin objects, which look like lacquered porcelain but are in fact papier mâché. This unique collection will never be copied: the Martin brothers died in Paris in the eighteenth century without disclosing the secret of their varnish. Before leaving, stroll through the grounds to the Pinetum, an imposing collection of California sequoias, cedars, Norway spruces, silver firs, and other conifers in a gorgeous setting.

PERTHSHIRE

Northeast of Perth towards Forfar. **Glamis Castle** (www.glamis-castle.co.uk; charge) was the childhood home of Queen Elizabeth

II, the Queen Mother, and the birthplace of the late Princess Margaret. Guided tours take in the fifteenth-century **crypt**, the family **chapel** and **Duncan's** Hall, a fifteenth-century guardroom. On the way to Glamis Castle, enthusiasts of archaeology might want to pause to look at the elaborately carved early Christian and Pictish monuments in the museum at **Meigle**.

Northwest of Perth is **Dunkeld**, with its restored 'little houses' from the seventeenth century. They lead to a once grand cathedral, standing amid tall trees, lawns, and interesting gravestones beside the River Tay, but now partly ruined, although the choir was renovated in the seventeenth century to serve as a parish church. The site was an ancient centre of Celtic Catholicism, and St Columba is said to have preached in a monastery on this site. Also note Thomas Telford's arched bridge (1809) over the Tay.

Blair Castle, seat of the Earls and Dukes of Atholl

Binoculars are provided at a fine wooden hide at the **Loch of the Lowes Wildlife Reserve**, two wooded miles (3km) from Dunkeld. Here, you can scan all kinds of water birds and study trees where ospreys nest after migrating from Africa.

At the hamlet of Meikleour, one of the arboreal wonders of the world lines the road: a gigantic **beech hedge**, which at about 100ft (30m) is the highest anywhere, planted in 1746 and still thriving.

Near Aberfeldy, once a Pictish centre, is the delightful little village of Fortingall on Loch Tay, with probably Scotland's finest thatched-roof cottages. It boasts the 'oldest living tree' in the United Kingdom, the **Fortingall Yew**, although there are other contenders. This ancient yew tree, surrounded by a rusty iron and stone enclosure in Fortingall's churchyard, is still growing and certainly doesn't look its presumed age – 5000 years. The hamlet is in Glen Lyon, the 'longest, loveliest, loneliest' glen in Scotland, according to the locals. Tranquillity reigns. Tradition has it – without scholarly confirmation – that Pontius Pilate was born in a nearby military encampment while his father was a Roman emissary to the Pictish king in the area.

Centrally located, the crowded summer resort of **Pitlochry** ⑭ is surrounded by dozens of attractions, both scenic and manmade. In the town itself, you might visit the Pitlochry Dam Visitor Centre (www.pitlochrydam.com; free) and Fish Ladder, where each year between five thousand and seven thousand salmon are counted electronically and watched through a windowed chamber as they make their way towards their spawning grounds. Pitlochry also has the well-regarded **Festival Theatre**.

A short drive west will bring you to the **Pass of Killiecrankie**, where you will want to walk along wooded paths to the spectacular parts of the gorge; here, too, is a National Trust centre which describes a particularly bloody battle between Jacobite and government forces in 1689. Just south, a roadside promontory known as the **Queen's View** commands a glorious sweep down along Loch Tummel and over Highland hills. On a good day this is among the best panoramas in Scotland.

North of Killekrankie, the white-turreted **Blair Castle** (www. atholl-estates.co.uk; charge), seat of the Earls and Dukes of Atholl, is a major tourist destination. The present duke commands Britain's only 'private army', a ceremonial Highland regiment of about sixty local riflemen and twenty pipers and drummers who march in their regalia very occasionally. The castle, which dates back seven hundred years but has been much reconstructed and restored, is crammed with possessions amassed by the Atholl family over the centuries: an extensive china collection, swords, rifles, antlers, stuffed animals and portraits. Look in particular for two rare colonial American powder horns, one with a map carved on it that shows forts and settlements around Manhattan Island, Albany, and the Mohawk River. Further west from Pitlochry is the long and thickly forested **Glen Garry**, one of Scotland's most wonderful mountain valleys. Be sure not to miss the **Falls of Bruar** cascading into the River Garry near the lower end of the glen.

ABERDEEN

The term 'granite city' is self-explanatory when you see the buildings sparkling in the sunshine at **Aberdeen ⓯**. Surprisingly, however, this solid metropolis, further north than Moscow, is anything but sombre: roses, daffodils and crocuses flourish in such profusion that the town has repeatedly won the Britain-in-Bloom trophy.

Scotland's third city is Europe's offshore oil capital, and was one of Britain's major fishing ports. The traditional fishing industry now has a small role to play in the economic life of the city and is mainly reduced to processing fish, while the actual fishing is centred round the port of Peterhead to the north. Most of the boats arriving in the harbour service the great oil rigs and platforms out at sea beyond the horizon. Aberdeen is Scotland's boom city, and its facilities have expanded to accommodate the influx of North Sea oil personnel, creating something of an international atmosphere for the many tourists who visit in the summer.

In the heart of the town, **Marischal College** is the second-largest granite building in the world after the Escorial in Spain. Built of a lighter-coloured variety known as 'white granite', it forms part of the complex of Aberdeen University. The city's first university, King's College, was founded in 1495. Dominating the pleasant quadrangle is the beloved local landmark, the Crown Tower of **King's Chapel**; knocked down in a storm in 1633, the structure was rebuilt with Renaissance additions. Inside the chapel, look for the arched oak ceiling, carved screen and stalls and Douglas Strachan's modern stained-glass windows.

Aberdeen's harbour

Nearby is the crowded graveyard of the oldest cathedral in Aberdeen, **St Machar's Cathedral** (www.stmachar.com; free), first built in 1357, and rebuilt in granite in the fifteenth century. Capping the marvellous stone interior with its stained-glass windows is a wonderful oak ceiling, bearing nearly fifty different coats of arms from Europe's royal houses and Scotland's bishops and nobles. One of Aberdeen's most interesting sites is **Provost Skene's House** (www.stmachar.com; free), which was built in 1545 making it the oldest private house in Aberdeen. Following a sensitive renovation, the house is now a superb museum, the highlight of which is the Hall of Heroes, featuring prominent people that are from, or who have had some association with, the city or area, for example the legendary former Aberdeen football manager Sir Alex Ferguson. The seventeenth-century **Mercat Cross**, ringed by a parapet engraved with the names of Scottish monarchs from James I to James VII, is claimed to be the finest example of a burgh (chartered town) cross to survive in Scotland. Aberdeen's charter dates back to 1179.

DUNNOTTAR CASTLE

South of Aberdeen, near Stonehaven, the vast ruins of **Dunnottar Castle** (www.dunnottarcastle.co.uk; charge) have had a rich and varied history. Here, in 1297, William Wallace burned alive an English Plantagenet

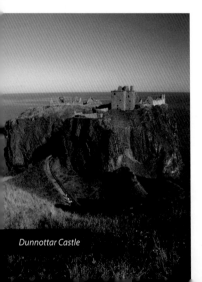
Dunnottar Castle

garrison. Much later, in 1650, the Scottish Crown Regalia were kept here during a siege by Oliver Cromwell's Roundheads. More recently, not to mention more peacefully, the film director Franco Zeffirelli used Dunnottar as the location for his film of *Hamlet*. Note: the steep steps down to the castle may be difficult for less mobile visitors.

ROYAL DEESIDE

The long, picturesque valley of the River Dee, extending inland from Aberdeen to the high Cairngorm Mountains, has been called **Royal Deeside** since Queen Victoria wrote glowingly about the area. Her 'dear paradise', **Balmoral Castle** (www.balmoralcastle.com; charge), about 41 miles (66km) west of Aberdeen, was purchased by Prince Albert in 1852 who refashioned the turreted mansion to his own taste in the Scottish Baronial style; the granite is local, and lighter than Aberdeen's. When the royal family is not in residence, several rooms are opened up to the public, as are the grounds. Across the road, modest Crathie Church is attended by the royal family.

Along the Dee near Aberdeen, **Crathes Castle** (www.nts.org. uk; charge) has some of Scotland's most dramatic gardens, with giant yew hedges that are clipped just once a year. The views from within the sixteenth-century tower-house over these remarkable hedges are in themselves worth the visit. Look also for the three rooms with painted ceilings, the carved-oak ceiling in the top-floor gallery, and the fourteenth-century ivory Horn of Leys, above the drawing-room fireplace.

THE HIGHLANDS

No longer really remote, the sparsely populated north of Scotland offers, above all, superb scenery as well as the country's most mysterious monster and most important distilleries.

THE RIVER SPEY AND THE MALT WHISKY TRAIL

For salmon and whisky, Scotland can offer you nowhere better than the **River Spey**. Along this beautiful valley of ferns and old bridges, you'll want to stop to watch anglers casting their long lines into the fastest-flowing river in the British Isles. Nestling among the trees are slate-roofed buildings with pagoda chimneys which produce the finest of all the fine Scotch whiskies, or so the local enthusiasts insist.

The Malt Whisky Trail (www.maltwhiskytrail.com) takes in nine distilleries, which includes one historic distillery and a cooperage, where you can watch malt being distilled by a process that has remained basically unchanged for five hundred years. You will usually be invited to enjoy a free wee dram. If you're lucky, at the Speyside Cooperage (www.speysidecooperage.co.uk; charge) you'll see a cooper (cask maker) fashioning oak staves into a cask: by law, a spirit can't be called 'whisky' until it has been aged in oak for three years. According to the experts, the best maturity for Scotch is about ten years.

Around the malt centre of Dufftown they still like to quote the saying: 'Rome was built on seven hills, Dufftown stands on seven stills' – although, at a recent count, there were in fact nine distilleries. Some of the best to visit are **Cardhu Distillery** in Knockando, **Glenfarclas** in Ballinalloch, **Glenfiddich** in Dufftown, **Glen Grant** in Rothes, **Glenlivet** in Glenlivet, and **Strathisla** in Keith.

THE NORTHEAST COAST AND INVERNESS

The northeast coast consists of a fertile coastal plain, shielded to the south by the Cairngorm Mountains. In the nineteenth century, this area was the centre of a fishing industry, and is dotted with many attractive fishing towns and villages, such as Buckie, Cullen and Portsoy. Just south of Lossiemouth, a fine fishing town and port, lies Elgin, a picturesque town that retains much of its medieval layout, with a cobbled marketplace and winding streets. The thirteenth-century **Elgin Cathedral** (www.historicenvironment. scot; charge) was once known as the 'Lantern of the North', and its ruins are still impressive.

In the Highlands, all roads lead to **Inverness** ⓰, capital of the Highlands since the days of the ancient Picts. It is worth stopping in this busy town to tour the small, modern **Museum and Art Gallery** (www.highlifehighland.com; free). In a fascinating exhibition of Scottish Highland history dating back to the Stone Age, you can brush up on your clan lore as well as inspect the dirks and sporrans, broadswords and powder horns.

LOCH NESS

Strategically situated where the River Ness joins the Moray Firth, **Inverness** is not at all shy about exploiting the submarine celebrity

Inverness

Urquhart Castle

Urquhart Castle
(www.historicenvironment.
scot; charge) sits by Loch
Ness between Fort William
and Inverness. Dating back
to the thirteenth century, the
castle played a key role in
the Wars of Independence,
being taken by Edward I and
later by Robert the Bruce.
Part of the building was
blown up in 1692 to prevent
it falling into Jacobite hands.

presumed to inhabit the waters of **Loch Ness** ⑰ to the south. Nessie T-shirts and all kinds of monster tat are on sale. Excursion boats offer regular monster-spotting cruises. You can cruise Loch Ness itself, and there are trips from the Caledonian Canal into Loch Ness (www.jaco-bite.co.uk).

Sonar and underwater cameras have been used by experts to close in on the mystery of the many sup-posed Nessie sightings, and most involved seem to agree that not one, but several large aquatic creatures might roam the murky depths of Loch Ness, surviving by eating eels and other fish.

Seven rivers feed this loch, bringing in millions of peat particles which reduce visibility to zero below 39ft (12m). At 23 miles (37km) long and about one mile (1.5km) across, Loch Ness is generally about 699ft (213m) deep – though in one area the silted bottom is nearly 1001ft (305m): enough space for a large family of mon-sters. The mysterious creature has intrigued people since it was first reported in the sixth century – by no less revered a traveller than St Columba.

On the busy A82, after leaving the loch, it is virtually impossible to miss the dramatic ruins of **Urquhart Castle** ⑱ (see page 72).

EAST OF INVERNESS

About five miles (8km) east of Inverness is **Culloden Battlefield** (www.nts.org.uk; charge), where Bonnie Prince Charlie's

Highlanders and the Jacobite cause were defeated by 'Butcher' Cumberland's redcoats in 1746. Jacobite headstones, a visitor centre and exhibition, a four-minute battle immersion film and a rooftop viewpoint recall this last major battle fought on British soil. Near the battlefield is the impressive archaeological site of **Clava Cairns**. Three once-domed tombs are encircled by standing stones. To stand in a silent burial chamber dating back to 1800 BC or 1500 BC is a slightly eerie experience.

Between Inverness and Nairn is **Cawdor Castle** (www.cawdor-castle.com; charge), a popular site set up to keep the visitor entertained; 'Three out of four Ghosts prefer Cawdor Castle', proclaims the sign at the castle's authentic drawbridge entrance. This fortress home of the Earls of Cawdor is the setting Shakespeare used for the murder of Duncan by Macbeth, although it was actually

The impressive Clava Cairns

A steep hike in the Cairngorms

constructed two centuries after Macbeth's time. The castle has all the features to make it a romantic focus: a drawbridge, an ancient tower and fortified walls. The 1454 tower's Thorn Tree Room is a stone vault enclosing a 600-year-old holly tree, while the castle grounds have outstanding flower and kitchen gardens, nature trails, and even a putting green. When you've seen the castle, head for nearby Cawdor village, with its delightful stone cottages set in beautifully tended gardens.

At Carrbridge the **Landmark Forest Adventure Park** (www.landmarkpark.co.uk) provides a wide range of outdoor activities for all the family.

Set against the spectacular backdrop of the Cairngorm Mountains, **Aviemore** ⓳ (see page 95) is one of country's main activity centres, with skiing in winter and hiking in summer the chief pursuits. The Cairngorms is one of only two in Scotland – the other being Loch Lomond and the Trossachs (see page 58), and whose massif is the UK's largest mountainscape and only sizeable plateau over 2500ft.

Some seven miles (11km) south, the excellent **Highland Wildlife Park** (www.highlandwildlifepark.org.uk; charge) at Kincraig has a drive-through area where you can get up close to vicuña, elk, bison and Przewalski's horses. Stars of the walk-through section include arctic foxes, red pandas, snow leopards and wildcats, while the park is also home to four of Britain's eight polar bears.

BEN NEVIS AND GLEN COE

The **Great Glen**, which follows the path of a geological fault, makes a scenic drive from Inverness south to Fort William. Near Fort William rises **Ben Nevis**, Great Britain's highest mountain, at 4406ft (1344m), although more often than not, clouds obscure its

Subtropical Inverewe Garden

rounded summit. The best view of the mountain is from the north, but it is most easily climbed from the west, starting near the bustling Highland touring centre of Fort William. Caution is advised here, as bad weather closes in quickly at the top of Ben Nevis and you can easily get lost.

From Loch Leven, historic **Glen Coe** cuts east through an impressive mountain range. Geology, flora, and fauna are illustrated at a visitor centre (www.nts.org.uk; free), and in the steep valley, you'll find a memorial to the 1692 massacre of the MacDonalds by the Campbell clan.

From Glen Coe and Fort William, you can take the famed **Road to the Isles**, with thoughts of Bonnie Prince Charlie in mind. The route goes past **Neptune's Staircase**, a series of eight lochs, designed by Thomas Telford as part of the Caledonian Canal. The road turns west to **Glenfinnan** (site of a memorial to fallen clansmen at the Battle of Culloden; see page 21) and north along the coast to **Morar**, with its white sandy beaches. One of Scotland's deepest lochs, Loch Morar, like Loch Ness, has its own monster, Morag. The end of the road is **Mallaig** [20], a little town with a picturesque harbour, where the ferry departs for Skye and other Hebridean islands.

THE NORTHWEST COAST

Near Dornie on the road towards Kyle of Lochalsh is the romantic and much-photographed **Eilean Donan Castle** (www.eileandonancastle.com; charge), connected to the land by a causeway. A Jacobite stronghold, it was destroyed by British warships, but was rebuilt in the nineteenth century. Three floors, including the banqueting hall, the bedrooms and the troops' quarters, are open to the public, with various Jacobite and clan relics also on display.

West from Inverness towards the coast, the dramatic Loch Torridon area is well known for its mountains of red-brown sandstone and white quartzite. These are some of the world's oldest mountains, probably six hundred million years old. The **Torridon Countryside Centre** in Torridon (www.nts.org.uk; Easter–Sept Sun–Fri 10am–5pm) offers guided walks in season.

The Gulf Stream works its magic at **Inverewe Garden ㉑** (www.nts.org.uk; charge), a subtropical oasis overlooking Loch Ewe, on the same latitude as Juneau, Alaska. The garden was started in 1862 by 20-year-old Osgood Mackenzie on 12,000 acres (4860 hectares) of barren land, and is one of the world's great plant collections. Late spring and early summer are the best seasons to visit; highlights include giant magnolias and the exotic Himalayan Hound's Tooth.

If you have time for a leisurely tour of Scotland's most spectacular scenery, turn north towards Ullapool. At a fine wooded

Ullapool, one of the prettiest villages on the west coast

spot just a few minutes' walk off the road below Loch Broom are the spectacular Falls of Measach, plunging 200ft (61m) into the **Corrieshalloch Gorge**.

Some of Scotland's most memorable scenery is along the jagged northwest coast above **Ullapool ㉒**, a fishing port and the ferry terminal for the Outer Hebrides. The secondary roads closest to the shore wind through beautiful country filled with mossy rocks, ferns, and hundreds of tiny lochans (small inland lochs). The first section goes through the **Inverpolly National Nature Reserve**. Near Lochinvar, strange stories gather around Suilven, the mount looming over the wild landscape (why don't animals graze on its slopes?). During the summer an excursion boat sets out from tiny Tarbet to **Handa Island**, a teeming bird sanctuary with huge sandstone cliffs and sandy beaches.

The Stacks of Duncansby

An early evening boat trip in Oban

Along Scotland's northern coast near Durness is **Smoo Cave** (free to access), which can be found in a beautiful setting at the end of a dramatic sea inlet. The 'gloophole' through the cathedral-like limestone roof of the large outer cavern gets its name from the noise made by air rushing up through it at high tide. Inside the second cave is a 79ft (24m) waterfall.

A lighthouse stands on **Dunnet Head**, a windy promontory on the northernmost point of the Scottish mainland, overlooking a forbidding sea. If there's no mist, Orkney is visible on the horizon. Nearby **John o'Groats** is far better known, although it isn't quite the most northerly tip of Great Britain.

The sign here declares it is 874 miles (1,406km) to Land's End in Cornwall, the greatest overland distance between any two points in Britain.

From Gills Bay, a few miles west of John o'Groats, you can take a ferry to the **Orkney Islands**, which have fascinating archaeological remains – including the Neolithic village of Skara Brae and the Ring of Brodgar.

Offshore from **Duncansby Head**, with its clifftop lighthouse, are the unusual pillar-like Stacks of Duncansby. Inland and to the south, make a short detour from the angling centre of **Lairg** to the Falls of Shin where, with luck, you will see sizeable salmon leaping up low, churning falls along the river.

THE INNER HEBRIDES

MULL

Peaceful moorland glens, sombre mountains, appealing shorelines and one of Scotland's prettiest ports are among the attractions of

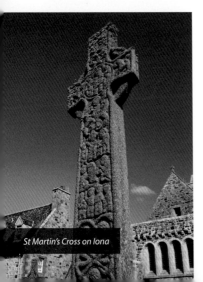
St Martin's Cross on Iona

the large western island of **Mull**. From **Oban** ㉓, the regular ferry takes 45 minutes to Craignure on Mull. The Tobermory ferry from Kilchoan takes about 35 minutes, and there is also an eighteen-minute ferry link between Fishnish Point and Lochaline across the Sound of Mull. In the summer, excursions go from Mull to several smaller islands, like Staffa and Lunga.

Tobermory ㉔ (pop. seven hundred), the island's delightful little capital, fits snugly in a harbour ringed

by forested hills and pro-
tected by flat, green Calve
Island. Regattas are held here
and golfers enjoy a splendid
seascape from the links just
above Tobermory.

In 1588 a gold-laden
galleon from the Spanish
Armada sank here, but sal-
vage efforts ever since have
failed. Calgary, to the southwest, which has probably the
best of Mull's sandy beaches, inspired the name of the Canadian
city about a century ago. If you're driving and not in a rush, take
the coastal road bordering Loch Na Keal; it's slow-going but scenic, along a single track beneath lonely cliffs and hills that are
mauve with heather.

Dozy sheep get out of your way reluctantly. Gaelic is still spoken here, particularly by the older generation. At the eastern
point, visible from the Oban ferry, stand Mull's two castles, both
open to the public.

Duart Castle (www.duartcastle.com; charge), on its promontory, guards the Sound of Mull. Dating back to the twelfth century,
Duart Castle is the home of the chiefs of clan Maclean, once a formidable sea power.

Johnson's verdict

When he visited Iona in the
year 1773, Samuel Johnson
wrote: 'That man is little to
be envied whose patriotism
would not gain force upon
the plain of Marathon, or
whose piety would not grow
warmer among the ruins
of Iona'.

IONA

The sacred island of **Iona** ㉕ lies just off the southwestern tip of
Mull. St Columba and about a dozen followers came from Ireland
to Iona in 563, bringing to Scotland the culture and learning of
the Celtic church, which spread through all of Europe. Some sixty
Scottish, Irish, French and Norwegian kings are buried on this

sacred island. Centuries of onslaughts by Vikings and others have left no trace of the earliest communities.

From Mull, Iona is reached via a one-track road and a ten-minute passenger ferry. Iona's fifteenth-century **abbey** (www.historicenvironment.scot; charge) restored virtually wholesale early last century. The three high crosses in front of the abbey date from the eighth to tenth centuries, and are decorated with the Pictish serpent-and-boss and Celtic spirals for which Iona's early Christian masons were renowned. Other sights are St Martin's Cross, carved in the tenth century; a small Norman chapel, built probably in 1072 by Queen Margaret; the attractive ruins of a thirteenth-century nunnery; and *Reilig Odhrain*, the graveyard where royalty, Highland chiefs, and more recent islanders are buried. Most of the older stones have been moved inside to preserve them from weather.

On a fine day, take a walk from here to North End where there are beaches of sparkling sand. Sheep, cattle and a few fishing boats indicate occupations, but in the summer most islanders – who live in the stone houses by the ferry landing – are involved with the throngs of visitors and pilgrims that arrive each year. From Iona you can take a boat trip to nearby **Staffa** island, which is home of the dramatic **Fingal's Cave**, a natural wonder which inspired part of Mendelssohn's *Hebrides Overture*. You can also get to Staffa from Mull or Oban.

SKYE

This busiest and best-loved Highland island is outrageously beautiful – whether the sun is shining or mists are swirling around its startling hills and idyllic glens. **Skye** is a thirty-minute ferry trip from Mallaig; otherwise, the Skye Bridge (toll free) links Kyleakin on Skye with Kyle of Lochalsh. **Portree** 26, with its colourful harbour, is the island's main town, and together with **Broadford**, these are the most popular centres for touring, but the island has many quieter places to stay.

The interesting and beautiful **Armadale Castle, Gardens & Museum of the Isles** ② (www.armadalecastle.com; charge) are sixteen miles (25km) south of Broadford, near the ferry terminal from Mallaig. For centuries the Macdonalds had styled themselves 'Lords of the Isles' and the museum has an exhibit detailing the history of the Highlands. The gardens and nature walks are outstanding.

Two remarkable ranges of peaks, the Black Cuillins in the south and the Quiraing in the north, make the island a hiker's or rock-climber's paradise (see page 93). Inside the wild and jagged **Cuillin Hills** is Loch Coruisk, which can be reached by boat from Elgol. Isolated by high peaks all around, the blue-black water of

Cuillin Hills viewed from Kyle of Lochalsh

Coruisk has an eerie beauty. The hamlets of Ord and Tarskavaig are worth visiting on a clear day for their splendid views of the Cuillins.

Dunvegan Castle ㉘ (www.dunvegancastle.com), northwest of Portree, has been the stronghold of the chiefs of MacLeod for more than seven centuries and is still the home of the chief of the clan. On display within this sturdy loch-side fortress is the Fairy Flag, a fragile remnant of silk believed to have been woven in Rhodes during the seventh century.

Supposedly, it saved the MacLeods in clan battles twice, and still has the power to do so one more time. Rather more down-to-earth is a pit dungeon – 13ft (4m) deep – into which prisoners were lowered from an upstairs chamber, though the grim aspect of the dungeon is somewhat diluted by a 'prisoner' and an audio of his groans. Samuel Johnson and James Boswell were entertained

Dunvegan Castle

here in 1773, and supplied with fresh horses to continue their journey.

From Dunvegan pier small boats make frequent half-hour trips to offshore rocks and islets to see the seals up close. The blubbery pinnipeds also appear, though less regularly, all around Skye's 998 miles (1609km) of coastline.

The dramatic collection of rocks known as the **Quiraing**, accessed more easily than the Cuillins,

Old Man of Storr

dominates the landscape north of the secondary road between Staffin and Uig, the ferry port for the Outer Hebrides. Reached by foot, the various rock features here include the castellated crags of the Prison, the slender 100ft (30m) Needle and the Table, a meadow as large as a football field.

Far north at Kilmuir are the grave and monument to Skye's romantic heroine, **Flora MacDonald**, who smuggled fugitive Bonnie Prince Charlie, disguised as her female servant, to safety. On the picturesque coast of Staffin, the Kilt Rock is a curiously fluted cliff with a waterfall that plunges down to the sea. Be extremely careful on this lofty ridge.

A mile further on, the Lealt Falls tumble down a long and accessible ravine into the sea at a pretty little cove. Salmon can sometimes be seen leaping here. Closer to Portree you will see a giant rock pinnacle called **Old Man of Storr**; there is a forest walk in the vicinity.

Throwing the hammer at the Perth Highland Games

THINGS TO DO

There's plenty to do wherever you might be staying in Scotland, particularly from spring to autumn. A range of information exists on the VisitScotland website (www.visitscotland.com) where you can also download brochures. The outdoors always beckons, and you'll stumble across many local happenings as you travel around.

ENTERTAINMENT

Most newsagents in Glasgow and Edinburgh stock *The List* (www.list.co.uk), a guide to upcoming events, theatre, cinema and clubs in both cities and their surrounding areas, which is published every two months.

SPECIAL EVENTS

Highland Games are staged all over the country during the summer months. In addition to kilted titans tossing a huge pine trunk – the famous caber – there'll be pipe and drum bands and accomplished shows of Highland dancing. The most famous of these events is the **Braemar Highland Gathering**, in early September, often attended by the reigning Monarch and members of the royal family, a custom started by Queen Victoria. Also of interest are the agricultural shows and sheepdog trials held in several farming areas.

Throughout the summer there are country fairs and many re-enactments of battles and other historic events. In July, the **Scottish Transport Extravaganza** at Glamis Castle, an exhibition of vintage vehicles, is the largest event of its kind in Scotland. **Ceilidhs**, or **folk nights**, which are held frequently in all parts of Scotland, feature dancers, pipers, fiddlers and a range of other artists, while folk festivals are staged in centres from Edinburgh to Stornoway. There has been a revival of Gaelic music and both the traditional and the modern-style music performed by groups like Capercaillie, Breabach and Salsa Celtica are enormously popular.

Of course, the most significant event of the year is the **Edinburgh International Festival**, which takes place in August. Virtuoso performances of music, opera, dance and theatre are staged by artists of international reputation; tickets are in great demand so book early both for tickets and hotel rooms. Even bigger is the **Edinburgh Festival Fringe**, which sees more than fifty thousand performances of over three thousand shows in almost three hundred venues. Other cultural high spots include Glasgow's **Celtic Connections Festival** and the **Wigtown Book Festival**.

Performing on the Royal Mile during the Edinburgh Festival

MUSIC AND THEATRE

The Theatre Royal in Glasgow is home to both the **Scottish Opera** and the **Scottish Ballet**, while the Glasgow Royal Concert Hall is the main venue for classical music, with regular concerts by the **Royal Scottish National Orchestra**. Both also perform regularly in Edinburgh, home to the prestigious Scottish Chamber Orchestra. The prestigious BBC Scottish Symphony Orchestra is based at City Halls in Glasgow, taking live music across the country. Churches in both cities regularly host excellent concerts.

Both cities have first-rate **theatre** scenes, with high-quality productions all year-round. The Citizens' Theatre in Glasgow presents serious drama, with more avant-garde shows at the Tramway

Festival fever

Also held during the Edinburgh Festival are the Military Tattoo and Book Festival, while other major summer events include the Art Festival (Aug) and the Jazz and Blues Festival (July).

and the Tron. In Edinburgh, the Traverse launches experimental work and the Royal Lyceum mounts a classical repertory. Shows, musicals and touring companies are also on the agenda. An important theatre season takes place over the summer in **Pitlochry** (see page 65). Other centres for regional theatre are St Andrews, Banchory, and Tobermory on Mull. Stirling's Tolbooth is a centre for the arts and music, and Big Burns festival in honour of Robert Burns takes place in Dumfries.

Major **music artists** appear at Hampden Park in Glasgow and Murrayfield Stadium in Edinburgh. Other main venues in Glasgow are the OVO Hydro and the Barrowland Ballroom. The **Glasgow International Jazz Festival** in June brings in jazz musicians from all over the world.

CLUBS AND PUBS

Pubs are very popular with the locals everywhere in Scotland and are especially crowded around the end of the working day and at weekends. The scene is lively and while the rowdy bar still exists, most pubs now have a relaxed and friendly atmosphere; many now also offer excellent food. Thanks to Scottish licensing laws, even children are welcome in many pubs. Many pubs in the cities also offer live music in the evening, and some, especially in Edinburgh, have their own resident folk or jazz musicians. In Glasgow, you can choose between traditional pubs and upmarket, fashionable bars. Café-bars are plentiful in both Glasgow and Edinburgh.

SPORT AND RECREATION

Scotland's outdoors attracts more visitors than its castles, museums or even the Edinburgh Festival.

FISHING

Scotland's rivers, lochs and coastal waters offer some of the finest game fishing in Europe. Much of it is free or very cheap; you don't need a general fishing licence, just a local permit. However, casting your line in the highly prized salmon beats costs hundreds of pounds per week, and you may have to book a year ahead for the privilege.

The **Spey**, **Tay** and **Tweed** are famous for salmon, sea trout and brown trout, though these fish also run in other Scottish waters. Most angling is fly; occasionally spinner or bait is permitted. If you'd like to learn the difference between a dry fly and an insect or how to stay upright while wading and casting in a rushing burn, experts are on hand all over Scotland. The VisitScotland website (www.visitscotland.

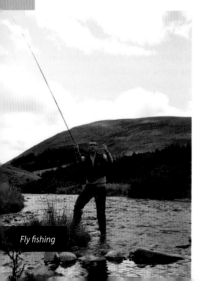
Fly fishing

com) and www.fishpal.com have information on fishing, with details of the best places, seasons and necessary permits. Fishing for salmon and sea trout is not allowed on Sundays and it is illegal for anglers to sell rod-caught salmon or sea trout. Coarse fishing for perch and pike is permitted year-round, including Sundays, and can be very good, particularly in southern waters.

Sea-angling trips run from ports along the Scottish coast and the islands; or you can fish from countless perches on the shore-line. Some species, such as dogfish and mackerel, can be found in abundance, and towards the end of the summer you might well hook blue or porbeagle shark.

For more information, contact the **Scottish Anglers National Association** (National Game Angling Centre, The Pier, Loch Leven, Kinross; www.sana.org.uk).

GOLF

Scotland is the original home of golf, a powerful lure for visitors wanting to play on the famous links. Many of Scotland's courses are municipal and open to everyone, but to play the famous courses, it helps to have a letter from your golf club at home stating your experience and handicap. If you choose your hotels or a special golfing-holiday package with care, you can play a different course each day of the week. The Scots make a distinction between two types of courses: links are on or near the sea; parkland (or heath-land) are inland, often on hilly terrain.

St Andrews, home of the **Royal and Ancient Golf Club** has seven courses of its own. Visitors with an ambition to play the historic **Old Course** should apply by phone or online (www.standrews.com) in August/September for the following year for a pre-booked tee-time, or enter the daily 'ballot', a lottery to determine which lucky applicants will fill vacancies and cancellations the next day. You can book any of the other St Andrews courses through the online booking system. Other outstanding Scottish golf courses include **Carnoustie**, **Royal Troon**, **Gleneagles**, **Muirfield**, **Royal Dornoch** and **Turnberry**.

BIKING, HIKING AND MOUNTAIN-CLIMBING

Biking. The Laggan Wolftrax Biking Centre (www.forestryandland. gov.scot/visit/laggan-wolftrax) near Newtonmore on the edge of the Cairngorms, is great for cycling enthusiasts, with more than twenty miles of routes for every standard. For more information about cycling, see the VisitScotland website: www.visitscotland. com/things-to-do/outdoor-activities/mountain-biking.

Hiking. Scotland's beautiful landscape offers unrivalled opportunities for hiking and hill walking. Most visited is the West Highland Way, which begins in Milngavie north of Glasgow and continues on past Loch Lomond up to Fort William, while the Southern Upland Way and Speyside Way are also popular long-distance footpaths. There are also many guided walks. In the Highlands, particularly, you will find nature walks and hill or plateau excursions led by trained naturalists; week-long hikes over moors and glens often include meals and accommodation in the price. At **Glen Coe** and

LINKS LINEAGE

When exactly golf began along the sandy coast in this chilly and windy land isn't clear, but the earliest record dates from 1457, when James II tried to outlaw golf as a menace to national security – too many Scots marksmen were skipping archery practice to swing at the little ball. Mary, Queen of Scots loved the game so much that she risked criticism by taking to the fairways while in mourning for her murdered husband. She is thought to have played at Bruntsfield in Edinburgh, probably the oldest course on which golf is still played today.

Torridon the National Trust for Scotland conducts several superb guided walks. VisitScotland (www.visitscotland.com/things-to-do/outdoor-activities/walking/routes-trails) has a range of walks on its website.

Mountain-climbing. You can take a strenuous walk up Britain's highest mountain, **Ben Nevis** (see page 75), climb the peaked ridges of the Isle of **Arran** (see page 48) or go rock climbing in the Black

Biking in the Cairngorms

Cuillins, depending on your skills. While their height is not great, the remote **Cuillins** on Skye offer some of the most challenging climbing in Britain (see page 83). **Mountaineering Scotland** in Perth (www.mountaineering.scot) can provide maps and telephone numbers to call for advice.

BOATING AND WATERSPORTS

Depending on your expertise, you can hire any sort of boat to explore Scotland's marvellous inland and coastal waters. **Sailing** schools offer courses for beginners all along Scotland's coast, and if you have documentation to prove your proficiency, you may be able to charter larger craft without a skipper.

Scotland is fast gaining a reputation as a top **surfing** destination, the best spots being Thurso, Tiree and the Isle of Lewis. **Windsurfing** and **kitesurfing** have also taken off, with Troon on the Ayrshire coast, St Andrews and Tiree the most popular

Climbing caveats

Despite a concentrated campaign for safety, mountain climbers continue to get into trouble in Scotland. Always get local advice on weather and conditions. Weather can change rapidly and suddenly, especially in the Highlands. Be sure you take the proper equipment and let someone know where you are going. Never go alone.

destinations. Summer days can be surprisingly hot, and swimming opportunities are abundant, but be alert for dangerous undertows and rip currents off western coasts.

The transparency of Scotland's waters makes them ideal for **scuba diving**. There are dive sites all around the coast, in various inland lochs and off the islands.

For further information on watersports in Scotland, see VisitScotland's website (www.visitscotland.com/things-to-do/outdoor-activities).

PONY TREKKING AND RIDING

All over Scotland there are horse and pony centres where you can ride by the hour, half-day or full day. Pony treks are led by expert guides, and many are suitable for young children; horseback trail riding is generally only for experienced riders. Some centres offer accommodation and weekly programmes with a different excursion each day. See the VisitScotland website (www.visitscotland.com/things-to-do/outdoor-activities/horse-riding-pony-trekking) for a list of reputable riding stables.

SKIING

Scotland has five major downhill ski centres: **Cairngorm** in Inverness-shire, **Glen Coe Mountain Resort** in Glen Coe, the **Nevis mountain range** in Inverness-shire, the **Lecht** and **Glenshee**, both in Aberdeenshire. The Cairngorms are Britain's highest mountains, and **Aviemore**, its centre, offers bus services to the ski areas, which have runs for skiers of all abilities. You'll find instructors, chairlifts, equipment hire, tows and accommodation at all the main ski areas; there's also the Cairngorm Mountain Railway. The ski season is December to May, though snowfall can be unpredictable (for updates: www.visitscotland.com/things-to-do/outdoor-activities/skiing-snowboarding).

SPECTATOR SPORTS

Rugby and football are as popular in Scotland as in the rest of the UK. Glasgow's Celtic and Rangers are the most successful soccer teams, while international matches take place in Hampden Park Stadium. Rugby's heartland is the Borders area, though both Glasgow and Edinburgh currently have successful teams. You may also want to observe the Scottish game of curling, a bit like bowling on ice, which has been practised in Scotland for at least four hundred years.

SHOPPING

Shops are generally open 9am–5.30pm Monday to Saturday (a few places may close on Saturday after-noon), and major shopping centres in cities are also open on Sunday. In the

Glasgow's Princes Square

Highlands, however, Sunday closing is generally the rule. In smaller towns, check whether there is an early closing day.

Glasgow is Scotland's major shopping city. Main areas are the smart, upmarket **Princes Square**, the Buchanan Quarter, and Ingram Street, known as Glasgow's style mile. Also popular is the St Enoch Centre, a huge glass structure. In Edinburgh the main shopping is on **Princes Street**, with most high street names, but for gifts, tartans and other Scottish wares, there are plenty of shops on the **Royal Mile**. For upmarket shopping, visit Multrees Walk just off St Andrew Square, and home to the likes of Harvey Nichols and Louis Vuitton. For vintage and boutique shops check out Stockbridge.

Almost all merchandise and services are subject to 20 percent **Value Added Tax (VAT)**. For major purchases over a certain amount of money, overseas visitors can get a VAT refund, but note that this applies only to shops that are members of the Retail Export Scheme. When you make your purchase, request a signed form and a stamped pre-addressed envelope; have your form stamped by British Customs as you leave the country and post the form back to the shop to obtain a refund. You can also avoid the VAT if you do your shopping in duty-free shops – look for the sign.

Visitors from EU countries should present the form to their home customs, who will insert the local VAT rate for the goods. This form should also be posted back to the shop for a refund.

WHAT TO BUY

Art and antiques. The Scottish art scene is an active one. Look for prints and affordable works by young Scottish artists. Victorian antiques and old prints and maps are also a good buy.

Crafts. In the Highlands you will find interesting stoneware and salt-glazed pottery. There are potters, jewellery-makers and other craftspeople on the Isles of Mull and Skye. Unusual 'heathergems' jewellery is made from stems of heather. Look out also for wood and stag-horn carvings, Celtic designs, handknits and handmade greetings cards.

Crystal. A number of high-quality glass and crystal producers have emerged from Scotland, including Caithness Glass, Selkirk Glass, Edinburgh Crystal and Stuart Crystal. There's also the Caithness Glass visitor centre in Crieff (www.caithnessglass.co.uk), where you can buy beautiful paperweights.

Kilts and tartans. A number of shops in Edinburgh, Glasgow, Stirling and Aberdeen specialise in made-to-measure kilts, or full Highland dress. These shops will be glad to help you find your family tartan.

Knitwear and woollens. Scottish knitwear includes cashmere pullovers and cardigans and Shetland and Fair Isle sweaters. Tartan woollens can be bought by the yard, and you can see them woven at several woollen mills. Harris tweed and sheepskin rugs are also popular buys.

Jewellery. In Glasgow (and elsewhere), look for sterling and enamel jewellery made from the designs of Charles Rennie Mackintosh. Silvercraft from Orkney and Shetland has designs inspired by Norse mythology. Celtic-designed jewellery, clan brooches and ornate kilt pins are often produced in pewter. And for the romantics there's the delicately worked luckenbooth, a traditional Scottish love token.

Dog and whisky in Edinburgh

Whisky. Scotch whisky is not necessarily less

Stargazing at the National Museum of Scotland

expensive in Scotland, but you'll find brands that you never knew existed, so take the opportunity to discover an unusual malt.

CHILDREN'S ACTIVITIES

Scotland has attractions and activities for children of all ages. Children enjoy exploring Scottish castles and there are many country parks with farm animals and playgrounds. Highland Games offer colourful spectacles with plenty of side shows (see page 87).

In Edinburgh, children might enjoy the Museum of Childhood on the Royal Mile (see page 34) and the National Museum of Scotland (see page 32). Older children will like the scary thrills of the **Edinburgh Dungeon** (www.thedungeons.com; charge). Both children and adults will find Our Dynamic Earth (see page 35) fascinating. **Edinburgh Zoo**, three miles (5km) from the centre, is Scotland's largest, on eighty acres (32 hectares) of hillside parkland (www.edinburghzoo.org.uk; charge).

In Glasgow, there's the **Scottish Football Museum** (www.scottishfootballmuseum.org.uk) at Hampden, where you can also take a tour of the stadium. At Coatbridge on the M8 motorway near Glasgow, the **Time Capsule** (www.activenl.co.uk/time-capsule-waterpark) offers fun for all with water chutes, ice skating and a soft play area.

CALENDAR OF EVENTS

January Celtic Connections, traditional music festival, www.celticco-nnections.com, Glasgow. 25 January: Burns Night, Scotland-wide. Last Tuesday in January: Up Helly Aa, fire festival, Lerwick, Shetland.

February Fort William Mountain Film Festival, for outdoor enthusiasts, www.mountainfilmfestival.co.uk.

March Glasgow International Comedy Festival, www.glasgowcomedy-festival.com. Fife Whisky Festival, showcasing the renaissance of whisky-making, www.fifewhiskyfestival.com.

April Edinburgh International Harp Festival, www.harpfestival.co.uk. Scottish Grand National, Ayr, www.scottishgrandnationalfestival.co.uk.

Late April–May Perth Festival of the Arts, www.perthfestival.co.uk. Dumfries & Galloway Arts Festival, www.dgartsfestival.org.uk, various venues.

June Common Ridings, festival of marking town boundaries on horse-back, Scottish Borders. WestFest, including the Festival Sunday Parade, Glasgow, www.westfest.uk. Royal Highland Show, farming event, Ingliston, near Edinburgh, www.royalhighlandshow.org. Glasgow International Jazz Festival, www.jazzfest.co.uk.

July Scottish Traditional Boat Festival, Portsoy, Aberdeenshire, www.stbfportsoy.org. Hebridean Celtic Festival, Celtic and grassroots artists perform, Isle of Lewis, www.hebceltfest.com. Edinburgh Jazz and Blues Festival.

August Edinburgh International Festival, www.eif.co.uk. Edinburgh Fringe Festival, www.edfringe.com. Edinburgh International Film Festival, www.eif.co.uk. Edinburgh Military Tattoo, www.edintattoo.co.uk. World Pipe Band Championship, with over two hundred bands, Glasgow.

September First Saturday: Braemar Highland Gathering, www.braemar-gathering.org. Doors Open Days, visit the country's best architecture for free, Scotland-wide, www.doorsopendays.org.uk.

October Royal National Mod, Gaelic language festival, different locations.

November 30 November (and week running up to it): St Andrew's Day.

December 31 December: Hogmanay, Scotland-wide.

FOOD AND DRINK

The Scots are very proud of the amount of good cooking to be found throughout their country, even in the remotest spots. Scottish chefs have won many accolades at international culinary competitions, and the better hotels and country house hotels may be staffed by award-winning chefs. Chefs are now keen to make full use of local ingredients: fresh salmon and trout, herring, beef, venison, grouse, pheasant, potatoes, raspberries and other fruit and vegetables. Oatmeal turns up in all kinds of dishes, but long gone are the days of Samuel Johnson's oft-quoted remark about oats after he toured the northern regions of Scotland: '…a grain which in England is generally given to horses, but in Scotland supports the people'.

Much Scottish fare is hearty, intended to act as a fortification against the weather. Whenever possible, try traditional dishes, which are often delicious. Vegetarian and vegan options are widely available in the cities, and are increasingly offered in smaller towns and villages.

Further info

The List's Eating and Drinking Guide provides listings for Edinburgh and Glasgow; www.list.co.uk. For restaurants serving traditional Scottish food visit www.taste-of-scotland. com.

WHEN TO EAT

Outside the main Scottish cities, restaurants, roadside inns and snack bars are rather thin on the ground. Even in the urban hubs, many of the finest Scottish restaurants are in hotels; non-residents are usually welcome, but check with guesthouses or smaller establishments. In the summer, it is a good idea to book a table in advance, particularly if the restaurant is known for its fine cuisine or helmed by a top chef.

If you are touring the remoter regions, picnic lunches are a good idea – you may find yourself miles from any food outlets, and there is certainly no shortage of lovely sites for outdoor feasts with a view.

Breakfast, usually from around 8am–10am, is provided by practically every

A full Scottish breakfast

hotel and guesthouse in Scotland. Away from major centres, restaurants may not serve lunch before noon or much after 2pm, and dinner may only be served in a short time window, such as between 7 and 9pm.

In general, restaurant prices compare favourably with those south of the border, although this does not prevent certain Scottish establishments from charging prices that would not be out of place in London's West End. Keep in mind the inclusion in restaurant prices of 20 percent VAT sales tax, and often a 10 percent service charge. A full Scottish breakfast is usually included in your hotel or bed and breakfast tariff.

While a light lunch at midday and more substantial dinner in the evening may be the style in tourist areas, conversely, in the countryside dinner is sometimes what the substantial midday meal is called, while the lighter evening meal may be called tea or supper.

WHAT TO EAT

Breakfast

Unlike England, where some hotels have converted to the 'continental breakfast', the Scottish breakfast still gives you the works. Porridge is served with cream or milk (and sugar, though this is frowned upon by traditionalists, who prefer salt and use water instead of milk), alongside fresh fruit and yoghurt, toast and jam, plus the option of a full cooked breakfast, typically consisting of eggs, sausage, bacon, tomatoes, mushrooms, potato scones and black pudding. A special touch is the addition of the Scottish kipper and smoked haddock – it's hard to argue with the conventional wisdom that Loch Fyne kippers are best, but it is equally hard to find a smoked herring from anywhere in Scotland that isn't delicious. The famous Arbroath smokies are salted haddock flavoured

---

SCOTCH BROTH

Traditional Scottish soups are best if they are home-made. Try a few of the following:

Cock-a-leekie – a seasoned broth made by boiling fowl with leeks and at times onions and prunes. Consumed for at least four hundred years and dubbed the national soup of Scotland.

Partan bree – creamed crab (partan) soup.

Scotch broth – a variety of vegetables in a barley-thickened soup with mutton or beef.

Cullen skink – milky broth of Finnan haddock with onions and potatoes.

Lorraine – a creamy chicken soup made with nutmeg, almonds and lemon, named after Mary of Guise-Lorraine.

Oatmeal – made with onion, leek, carrot and turnip.

Try Arbroath smokies while in Scotland

with hot birch or oak smoke. Finnan haddock (or haddie) are salted and smoked over peat. Pâtés of kipper, trout, smoked salmon and haddock have become favourite starters in good restaurants.

Main courses

Fish and shellfish. Scottish smoked salmon is famous all over the world, thanks to the special flavours introduced by the distinctive peat or oak-chip smoking process. Farmed salmon is now widely available, and while the purist may argue that it isn't as good as the wild variety, there are few people who can actually tell the difference between the two.

Nothing is better than a whole fresh salmon poached with wine and vegetables. The west coast is renowned for the excellence of its lobster, scallops, crayfish, mussels and oysters.

Meat and game. Scottish beef rivals the best in Europe. Aberdeen Angus steak is a favourite, served with a mushroom-and-wine

Haggis and whisky

sauce. Whisky flavours many a sauce served with beef: Gaelic steak, for instance, is seasoned with garlic and fried with sautéed onions, with the spirit added during the cooking process. Whisky is also used in preparing seafood, poultry and game. *Forfar bridies* are pastry puffs stuffed with minced steak and onions. If you are lucky, you might also find beef collops (slices) in pickled walnut sauce. Veal is rather scarce. In recent years, lamb has appeared more frequently, sometimes in ingenious dishes. Game still abounds in Scotland. After the shooting season opens (on the 'glorious 12th' of August), grouse is an expensive but much sought-after dish, served in a pie or roasted with crispy bacon and paired with bread sauce or fried breadcrumbs. Venison appears frequently on the menu, often roasted or in a casserole. You will also find pheasant, guinea fowl, quail and hare in terrines, pâtés and game pies.

Haggis. Haggis, Scotland's national dish, hardly deserves its horrific reputation among non-Scots. Properly made, it consists of chopped-up sheep's innards, oatmeal, onions, beef suet and seasoning, boiled in a sewn-up sheep's stomach bag. Haggis is traditionally accompanied by *chappit tatties* and *bashed neeps* – mashed potatoes and turnips.

Other traditional dishes include Scotch eggs: hard-boiled eggs coated with sausage meat and breadcrumbs, deep-fried and eaten hot or cold. Scotch woodcock is toast topped with anchovy and scrambled egg.

Potatoes and oatmeal. Potatoes are a particular local pride. *Stovies* are leftovers from the Sunday roast, usually including potatoes, onions, carrots, gravy and occasionally the meat, cooked in the dripping. *Rumbledethumps* are a mixture of boiled cabbage and mashed potatoes (sometimes with a sprinkling of onions or chives and grated cheese). You should not have to go all the way to northernmost Caithness for Scotland's basic dish of *tatties* (potatoes boiled in their skin) and herrings. And in the Orkney Islands, a local favourite is *clapshot* (potatoes and turnips mashed together and seasoned with fresh black pepper), the best accompaniment for their haggis.

Afternoon tea, dessert and cheese

Tea rooms all over Scotland offer afternoon tea, with sandwiches, cakes and other delicacies. Shortbread is, of course, a Scottish speciality. Another classic Scottish speciality is rich, dark Dundee cake, made with dried fruits and spices and topped with almonds. Dundee also contributed bitter orange marmalade to the world in the 1700s.

Scones and bannocks (oatmeal cakes) are among the great array of Scottish baked and griddled goods. A teatime treat is Scotch pancakes, served with butter and marmalade or honey. Oatcakes come either rough or smooth and they are eaten on their own or with butter, pâté, jam or crowdie, Scotland's centuries-old version of cottage cheese. In Edinburgh, the afternoon tea

Skirlie

Skirlie is a mixture of oatmeal and onions flavoured with thyme. Oatmeal also turns up as a coating on such foods as herring and cheese and in desserts.

at the *Balmoral Hotel* is famous, and in Glasgow, don't miss going to the *Willow Tea Rooms*, recreated from the original designs of Charles Rennie Mackintosh.

For dessert, you'll see various combinations of cheese, with red berries or black cherries and vanilla ice cream. Cranachan, a tasty Scottish speciality, consists of toasted oatmeal and cream and whisky or rum topped with nuts and raspberries or other soft fruit. Rhubarb-and-ginger tart is worth looking out for, as is butterscotch tart.

Scotland produces several excellent varieties of cheddar cheese and recent years have seen a rediscovery of old Scottish cheeses. Produced (although on a small scale) throughout the country, the speciality cheeses are characterised by a high degree of individuality. Try Criffel, Lanark blue, Isle of Mull or creamy Crannog or Orkney Cheddar.

WHAT TO DRINK

A huge amount of folklore surrounds every aspect of **Scotch whisky**, from its distillation using pure mountain water, to the aroma of the peat, to its storage, all the way to the actual drinking. The word 'whisky' derives from the Gaelic *uisge beatha* or 'water of life'. It is available in two basic types – malt (distilled solely from malted barley) and grain (made from malted barley and grain). Most of the Scotch sold today is blended, combining malt and grain whiskies. There are now more than two thousand brands of authentic Scotch whisky.

The malt whiskies come primarily from Speyside and the Highlands, and each has its own distinctive flavour: dry, smoky, peppery, peaty or sweet. Purists insist that a single-malt whisky should be drunk only neat or with plain water – never with other mixers, although these are acceptable with blended Scotch, even by Scots.

Glenmorangie distillery

After dinner, Scotland's version of Irish coffee, which naturally uses local whisky, may be called a 'Gaelic coffee'. A rusty nail, believed for obvious reasons to have associations with a coffin nail, is one measure of malt whisky plus one measure of Drambuie. A 'Scotch mist' is made from whisky, squeezed lemon rind and crushed ice, shaken well. An 'Atholl Brose' blends oatmeal, heather honey and whisky.

Because of the country's long-standing association with France, good French **wine**, especially claret, was on Scottish tables before it was widely available in England. Most hotels and restaurants offer an extensive wine list, often now including good varieties from New Zealand, Australia and Chile.

Scotland is proud of its **beer**. The Scottish equivalent of English 'bitter' is called 'heavy', and should be served at room temperature. The 'half and a half' featured in old-fashioned pubs is a dram of whisky with a half-pint of beer as a chaser.

WHERE TO EAT

We have used the following symbols to give an idea of the price for a three-course meal for one person without wine or service.

££££	over £50
£££	£35–£50
££	£25–£35
£	under £25

EDINBURGH AND LOTHIAN

Champany Inn £££ *Linlithgow, West Lothian,* www.champany.com. Acclaimed for its steaks and wine cellar, and set in an old mill with beamed ceilings and antique tables. An informal, moderately priced 'Chop and Ale House' adjoins. Reservations advised.

Contini Ristorante ££ *103 George Street,* www.contini.com. The name may have changed at *Centotre,* as it was formerly known, but the same family still serve the same delicious northern Italian food with the freshest seasonal produce, for example tortellini stuffed with ricotta and East Lothian crab.

L'Escargot Bleu ££ *56 Broughton Street,* www.lescargotbleu.co.uk. This engaging restaurant is very French, from the red-chequered tablecloths and posters on the wall to the warm and welcoming staff. Classic French country cooking is brought to bear on a range of locally sourced produce, as in the pan-fried venison with its own pie, heaps of braised red cabbage and apple sauce.

Gusto ££ *135 George Street,* www.gustorestaurants.uk.com. A typical trattoria with a modern twist: open kitchen, stainless-steel decor, and a bustling atmosphere combined with traditional Italian cooking.

Howies ££ *29 Waterloo Place,* www.howies.uk.com. Elegant Georgian setting to enjoy Scottish and French cuisine consisting of fresh, tasty ingredients in an informal atmosphere.

Kalpna ££ *2–3 St Patrick Square,* www.kalpnarestaurant.com. Outstanding vegetarian family restaurant that's been serving authentic Gujarati dishes in town for over 25 years. Superb *thaalis*, including a vegan option, stand alongside the main menu for those keen to sample a range of dishes.

The Kitchin ££££ *78 Commercial Quay,* www.thekitchin.com. The motto at this Michelin-starred restaurant is "from nature to plate", a philosophy that ensures the freshest ingredients, particularly well demonstrated on its "Celebration of the Season" menu that might include hand-dived Orkney scallops or roast Highland wagyu beef.

Number One ££££ *The Balmoral Hotel, 1 Princes Street,* www.roccoforte hotels.com. World-class cooking, using the very best of fresh, seasonal Scottish produce, at this wonderfully stylish restaurant inside the equally plush *Balmoral Hotel*.

Pickles £ *56a Broughton Street,* www.getpickled.co.uk. For something different and a little lighter, this chilled-out place offers delicious platters groaning beneath the weight of Scottish cheeses or local meats and, naturally, a huge range of pickles and sides.

Timberyard £££ *10 Lady Lawson Street,* www.timberyard.co. Located in a former warehouse, this gorgeously rustic restaurant focuses on high-quality Scottish produce, some of it home-grown or smoked on site; much of the rest is sourced from local foragers or farmers directly.

The Witchery by the Castle ££££ *352 Castlehill, Royal Mile,* www.thewitchery. com. Whether it is Aberdeen Angus beef or Scottish lobster, the cooking at *The Witchery by the Castle* won't disappoint – and a galaxy of celebrities would agree. A good table d'hôte menu helps to keep the cost down.

SOUTH AND BORDERS

Fox & Willow ££ *46 Carrick Road, Ayr,* www.thefoxandwillow.co.uk. This hotel restaurant delivers great service along with a mouth-watering combination of flavours. Slow-cooked beef cheek is a popular starter, as is grilled fillet of seabass with langoustine for mains.

Kailzie Gardens Courtyard Café £ *Near Peebles (on the B7062)*, www.kailzie gardens.com. This delightful café serves wholesome home-cooked lunches – including a superb Sunday roast – and fine afternoon teas inspired by local suppliers. Booking advised.

Marmions Brasserie ££ *Buccleuch Street, Melrose, The Borders*, www.marmions brasserie.co.uk. A good place to stop for lunch when touring the Border abbeys, this relaxed, friendly restaurant makes good use of local produce, such as Scottish lamb casserole with market veg.

Simply Scottish £ *6–8 High Street, Jedburgh, Roxburghshire, tel: 01835-864696.* A café that serves sophisticated and contemporary Scottish fare, made from the freshest ingredients.

GLASGOW

Babbity Bowster ££ *16–18 Blackfriars Street*, www.babbitybowster.com. The popular downstairs café-bar serves seafood and Scottish fare with a French influence, but for a quieter, more intimate dinner, it's advisable to eat upstairs in the charming dining room (dinner only Friday–Saturday). You can stay here too, but it can get noisy.

Café Gandolfi £££ *64 Albion St*, www.cafegandolfi.com. In the heart of Glasgow's merchant city, this snappy restaurant serves up a wonderful selection of Scottish-inspired dishes, such as peat-smoked salmon, and seared Barra scallops with Stornoway black pudding.

Cail Bruch ££££ *725 Great Western Street*, www.cailbruch.co.uk. Glasgow's first Michelin-starred restaurant offering dazzling five- and seven-course tasting menus. Expect inventive plates like Gigha halibut with Jerusalem artichoke and beurre noisette, and Orkney scallops with crème fraîche and sauce albuféra.

Drum and Monkey £ *91 St Vincent Street*, www.nicholsonspubs.co.uk. This casual pub-restaurant serves excellent Scottish-French cuisine in inviting Victorian surroundings alongside an unbeatable whisky menu – very much a local favourite.

La Lanterna ££ *447 Great Western Road,* www.lalanterna-glasgow.co.uk. This small, unpretentious establishment in Glasgow's west end serves Italian cuisine in elegant, contemporary surroundings. The pre-theatre menu is excellent value.

Ox and Finch ££ *920 Sauchiehall Street,* www.oxandfinch.com. In a trendy part of town, this sharing-plate restaurant offers relaxed and rustic fine dining. The menu consists of a selection of tapas dishes, and the dining area is bright and open.

Red Onion ££ *257 West Campbell Street,* www.red-onion.co.uk. Dishes are a modern twist on classic Scottish cooking, all delicately prepared. The spacious and relaxed space has mixed seating, including booths and a mezzanine.

Willow Tea Rooms £ *97 Buchanan Street,* www.willowtearooms.co.uk. This is a faithful re-creation of the innovative design work Mackintosh carried out for restaurateur Kate Cranston at the turn of the twentieth century. As delicious as the food is here, it's really all about the fabulous afternoon tea in stunning surroundings.

Windows ££ *In the Carlton George, 44 West George Street, 7th floor,* www.carlton.nl/george. An excellent and attractive restaurant with sensational rooftop views. Only the freshest produce is used in dishes that celebrate Scottish cuisine. It is advisable to book.

Yiamas £ *16–20 Bath Street,* www.yiamas-greek-taverna.co.uk. A basic but homely Greek tavern serving authentic food from its open kitchen. The Greek owners really bring out the flavour in dishes on the meze-style menu, such as giros, stifado and moussaka.

CENTRAL SCOTLAND

But 'n' Ben ££ *Auchmithie,* www.thebutnben.com. This restaurant, housed in an attractive row of cottages, is best known for its high tea and inexpensive seafood dishes, served in comfortable surroundings by friendly and attentive staff.

The Cellar £££ *24 East Green, Anstruther, Fife*, www.thecellaranstruther.co.uk. This famed seafood restaurant in the waterfront town of Anstruther is still in touch with old practices such as drying, salting, fermenting and smoking. Excellent wine list.

Clachan Inn £ *2 Drymen Square, Drymen*, www.clachaninndrymen.co.uk. Colourful, characterful eighteenth-century inn with a decent pub menu comprising the likes of Malaysian lamb casserole, as well as pizzas. Very child-friendly, with special kids' menu.

India on the Green £ *9 Victoria Road, Ballater, tel: 01339-755701*. For delicate cuisine from India and Bangladesh with a Western twist, try this award-winning option.

The Kilberry Inn ££ *Kilberry Road, Kilberry*, www.kilberryinn.com. It's worth seeking out this wonderful restaurant-with-rooms, reached by a single-track road between Tarbet and Lochgilphead. The local produce is used to excellent effect, resulting in delicious dishes like seared Jura king scallops, and wild venison wellington.

Moon Fish Cafe £££ *9 Correction Wynd, Aberdeen*, www.moonfishcafe. co.uk. Tucked away among Aberdeen's medieval streets, the changing menu brings up-and-coming food trends from around the world to the table. Friendly staff create an unpretentious atmosphere.

Old Boatyard ££ *Fishmarket Quay, Arbroath*, www.oldboatyard.co.uk. This inviting restaurant is set in an attractive modern building with a traditional feel in Arbroath's modern harbour. Seafood is a favourite, but there are plenty of other tasty choices.

Peat Inn ££££ *By Cupar, Fife*, www.thepeatinn.co.uk. A pioneer in the revival of Scottish cuisine, this Michelin-starred restaurant is a dining experience beyond most in Scotland. Reservations recommended. If you want to stay here as well, the inn has eight rooms; book well in advance.

The Seafood Restaurant ££££ *Bruce Embankment, St Andrews*, www.the seafoodrestaurant.com. Where better to eat the likes of lobster raviolo, East

Neuk crab with smoked eel, and Orkney scallops than in this classy restaurant with a beautiful view over the water.

The Silver Darling £££ *Pocra Quay, Aberdeen,* www.thesilverdarling.co.uk. Superb seafood that varies depending on that day's catch, but the platters offer a fabulous nibble of everything. 'Silver Darling' is the local nickname for herring.

HIGHLANDS AND ISLANDS

Badachro Inn ££ *By Gairloch,* www.badachroinn.com. Delightful setting overlooking Loch Gairloch for this popular pub with a pleasant garden. The daily changing menus highlight locally caught seafood, and there is a wide choice of real ale, wine or malt whisky.

Café 1 ££ *75 Castle Street, Inverness,* www.cafe1.net. Located in the town centre, this well-reputed restaurant offers new Scottish cuisine such as rump of Highland lamb with *skirlie* potatoes and black-pudding bon bons. Reservations recommended.

Dulse & Brose £££ *In the Bosville Hotel, Portree, Skye,* www.perlehotels.com. Serving bistro-style food where fresh local seafood is a speciality. The dishes are seasoned with locally grown herbs and accompanied by organic vegetables. Reservations essential.

Old Pier Café £ *Lamlash, Arran,* www.oldpiercafe.com.uk. This little retro tearoom offers hearty breakfasts, a good selection of hot and cold lunch options and delicious cakes. It does get extremely busy so you might have to wait for a seat.

The Three Chimneys ££££ *Colbost (near Dunvegan), Skye,* www.three chimneys.co.uk. The undisputed culinary heavyweight of Skye. Head chef Scott Davies draws on the natural larder of the Scottish Highlands and Islands to create exquisite dishes for discerning diners. Book the Kitchen Table experience for a first-row seat to the culinary theatre. Expect the likes of cold smoked trout with truffle, and roasted partridge with plum ketchup. Five-star rooms also available for overnight stays. Reservations essential.

TRAVEL ESSENTIALS

PRACTICAL INFORMATION

A

ACCESSIBLE TRAVEL

Capability Scotland is Scotland's leading disability organisation, providing a range of flexible services which support disabled people of all ages in their everyday lives. Contact: Capability Scotland, Osborne House, 1 Osborne Terrace, Edinburgh EH12 5HG (www.capability.scot).

ACCOMMODATION (see also Camping, Youth hostels and Recommended hotels)

There is a great variety of accommodation in Scotland, including hotels, guesthouses, manor houses, castles and bed-and-breakfasts (B&Bs), many of which are graded by VisitScotland. There are also hundreds of self-catering cottages, caravans, chalets and crofts (small farmhouses), plus campsites. Farmhouse holidays and accommodation in private homes are other possibilities.

VisitScotland (www.visitscotland.com) has a comprehensive list of accommodation, including establishments that have facilities for disabled visitors and young children.

Hotels vary greatly in standards; many of the most pleasant are converted country mansions in isolated settings. Some hotels have swimming pools, and a few even have their own golf courses. Guesthouses and B&Bs can be great value, although you'll sometimes have to share a bathroom. Most establishments have a restaurant or can arrange for an evening meal.

Book ahead for Easter, and July–September. Some tourist offices offer 'local bed-booking' services that assure overnight accommodation on the same day. You pay a minimal deposit for the reservation, which is deducted from your bill. Some tourist boards also charge a small booking fee.

AIRPORTS

Scotland has four major airports – Glasgow, Edinburgh, Inverness and Aberdeen – in addition to many regional airports scattered about on the mainland and the islands that are served by Loganair.

Glasgow Airport (www.glasgowairport.com) handles UK, European and transatlantic services. It is a nine-mile (15km), twenty-minute taxi or bus ride from the city centre. Buses, including the Glasgow Airport Express (#500), travel every ten to twenty minutes between the airport and Buchanan bus station in central Glasgow. Buses from Buchanan station travel to Edinburgh (1hr 10min) and other destinations in Scotland.

Edinburgh Airport (www.edinburghairport.com) also handles UK, European and transatlantic services. The airport is seven miles (11km) from Edinburgh, and is linked with Waverley railway station at Waverley Bridge, in the city centre by a special Airlink bus service (#100) that leaves every ten minutes and takes about thirty minutes. A tram runs from the airport to the city centre and onwards to Newhaven. Taxis are available just outside the arrival hall.

Inverness Airport (www.hial.co.uk/inverness-airport), seven miles (11km) east of the city in Dalcross, handles mostly British flights, including to many of the Scottish islands, and a few European flights. The airport has its own train station and there are buses (ever 30min) into the city centre.

Aberdeen Airport (www.aberdeenairport.com), a seven-mile (11km), 35-minute bus ride from Aberdeen station, serves mainly Britain and Europe.

B

BICYCLE HIRE

Scotland offers many cycling opportunities, and you'll find **bike rental** facilities in all large towns and tourist centres; expect to pay around £20 per day. although bikes can usually also be rented by the hour, half-day or week. Book ahead for July or August. See page 92 for information about biking trails.

BUDGETING FOR YOUR TRIP

Although good value for money is still the general rule in Scotland, bargains are rare and inflation relentlessly does its familiar work.

Accommodation: Double in moderately priced hotel with breakfast, £60–70 per person. Double in guesthouse with breakfast £40–60 per person. Bed-and-breakfast (without bath), £35–50 per person.

Airport transfer: Edinburgh: bus £5.50 (£8 return), tram £7, taxi about £25. Glasgow: bus (Glasgow Express) £8.50 (£14 return), taxi £25.

Bicycle hire: £20–30 per day, £70–90 per week.

Buses: Edinburgh–Glasgow (standard tickets) £9.90 (£15.50 return). Explorer Pass: 3 days within five consecutive days £60; 5 days within ten consecutive days) £89; www.citylink.co.uk. City and local buses: fares can depend on distance. Minimum bus fare in Edinburgh is £2, and £5 for a day ticket. Glasgow bus fares start at £2, and a day pass costs £5.40; exact fare is required.

Campsites: £15–25 per tent per night.

Meals: Lunch in pub or café £12–18; moderately priced restaurant meal with wine £25–35; afternoon tea £12; a pint of beer £4–5.50.

Shopping: Pure wool tartan around £46 per metre; cashmere scarf from £35; kilt: man's from £250, woman's from £125; cashmere sweater from £100; lambswool sweater £25–40.

Sights: Many national museums, as well as some National Trust and Historic Environment Scotland sights, are free; for other sights expect to pay anywhere between £5 and £19.

Taxis: Basic rate (Edinburgh) for two passengers begins at £2.10; increases by 25p every 210m/yds until 11.30pm, then for every 242m/yds; 20p extra for each additional passenger.

Tours: City on-and-off bus tours £16; sightseeing day tours from £18; cruises from one hour to full day £15–40.

Trains: Prices vary according to day or time of travel. Sample one-way off-peak fares include Glasgow–Edinburgh £14.70, Glasgow–Aberdeen £22.50, Edinburgh–Inverness £26 (www.scotrail.co.uk). Spirit of Scotland pass (accepted on trains, buses and most ferries): 8 days (4 days of travel) £149, 15 days (8 days of travel) £189.

C

CAMPING

There are more than six hundred campsites in Scotland, most of which have hot showers, flush toilets and laundry facilities, and often shops too. Other sites are more basic, with just a handful of pitches. Unlike other areas of Britain, wild camping is permitted in Scotland, just so long as it is done responsibly; check out www.outdooraccess-scotland.scot.

VisitScotland has a list of sites (www.visitscotland.com/accommodation/caravan-camping), while some of the most attractive locations are operated by Forestry and Land Scotland (www.forestryandland.gov.scot).

CAR HIRE

As a rule, it is cheaper to book a hire car before you leave on your trip. Be sure to check whether your credit card covers insurance. A medium-sized compact family car will cost around £240 per week, £48 per day, including VAT, unlimited mileage, but not insurance. Prices vary widely according to season. Beware hidden extras.

To hire a car you must be 21 or over and have held a driver's licence for at least twelve months. Valid drivers' licences from almost all countries are recognised by the British authorities.

Major car rental companies are: Avis (www.avis.co.uk); Budget (www.budget.co.uk); Europcar (www.europcar.co.uk); Hertz (www.hertz.co.uk). For competitive rates, try Arnold Clark (www.arnoldclarkrental.com).

CLIMATE

The best months to visit Scotland are May and June, which have the most hours of sunshine and comparatively little rain. There aren't many of the midges and other stinging insects that become a problem, especially on the west coast, in full summer.

Average monthly temperatures are as follows:

	J	F	M	A	M	J	J	A	S	O	N	D
°C	4	5	7	10	14	17	19	18	15	11	7	6
°F	39	41	44	50	58	62	66	64	59	52	44	43

CLOTHING

Even if you're holidaying in Scotland in midsummer, take warm clothing and rainwear. Anoraks are very useful: buy a bright colour to make yourself conspicuous to hunters if you're going to be hiking or climbing. Sturdy shoes are a must both for outdoor walking and traversing cobblestone streets.

Scotland makes some of the world's best clothing, and you'll find a fine selection of knits, woollens and tweeds, although not at significantly lower prices than elsewhere in the UK.

CRIME AND SAFETY

As everywhere, crime in Scotland can be a problem, but even Glasgow, with Scotland's highest crime rate, is not dangerous by world standards. Take all the usual precautions.

D

DRIVING

Road conditions. A limited number of motorways connect Glasgow and Edinburgh with other major cities and areas. Be aware that most A roads are winding, two-lane roads, often skirting Scotland's many lochs and they can be slow-going. A surprise to most visitors are the single-lane roads found in the hinterland and on the islands. Most of these are paved, with passing places for giving way to oncoming traffic or allowing cars behind you to overtake (thank the driver who pulls over for you); you should never park in these essential passing places. The twisting roads, along with the need for pulling in and out of the side slips, will more than double your normal driving time even over short distances. Other obstacles include sheep and cattle that often wander onto minor roads.

Rules and regulations. The same basic rules apply in all of Britain. Drive on the left, overtake on the right. Turn left on a roundabout (traffic circle); at a junction where no road has priority, yield to traffic coming from the right. Seat belts must be worn. Drinking and driving is regarded as a serious offence and penalties are severe, involving loss of licence, heavy fines, and even prison sentences, and the law is strictly enforced.

To bring a car into Scotland you'll need registration and insurance papers and a driver's licence. Overseas visitors driving their own cars will need Green Card insurance as well.

Speed limits. In built-up areas, 30 or 40mph (48 or 65kmh); on major roads, 60mph (96kmh); on dual carriageways and motorways, 70mph (112kmh).

Fuel. Petrol is sold by the Imperial gallon (about 20 percent more voluminous than the US gallon) and by the litre; pumps show both measures. Four-star grade is 97 octane and three-star is 94 octane. Unleaded petrol and diesel is widely available, and most petrol stations are self-service. In the more remote areas, however, stations are rather scarce, so take advantage whenever you see one.

If you need help. Members of automobile clubs that are affiliated with the British Automobile Association (AA) or the Royal Automobile Club (RAC) can benefit from speedy, efficient assistance in the event of a breakdown. If this should happen to you, AA members should tel: 0800-887 766, RAC members tel: 0800-828 282. Green Flag Motoring Assistance, tel: 0800-051 0636.

Parking. There are parking meters in major centres and vigilant corps of traffic police and wardens to ticket violators, even in small towns. Ticket machines take most coins and some now take credit cards. Do not park on double yellow lines.

In Edinburgh and Glasgow, your car is best left in a car park. Concert Square, next to Buchanan bus station in Glasgow, has a large multistorey car park. In Edinburgh, Castle Terrace is a large multistorey car park near Edinburgh Castle; St James' Centre (enter on York Place) is at the east end of Princes Street.

Road signs. Many standard international picture signs are displayed in Scotland. Distances are shown in miles. In the Highlands and Islands only, road signs may appear first in Gaelic, then English.

E

ELECTRICITY

Throughout Scotland it's 230 volts AC, 50 Hz. Certain appliances may need a converter. Americans will need an adapter.

EMBASSIES AND CONSULATES

Many countries have consuls or other representatives in Edinburgh, but others only have representation in London.

Australia: Australian High Commission, Australia House, Strand, London WC2B 4LA, tel: 020 7379 4334, www.uk.embassy.gov.au.

Canada: Canadian Consulate, tel: 07702 359916, email: canada.consul.edi@gmail.com.

US: American Consulate General, 3 Regent Terrace, Edinburgh EH7 5BW, tel: 0131-556 8315, www.uk.usembassy.gov

EMERGENCIES

To call the fire brigade, police, ambulance, coast guard, lifeboat, or mountain rescue service, dial 999 from any telephone. You don't need a coin. Tell the emergency operator which service you need.

G

GETTING THERE

By air.

From North America. Direct transatlantic flights to Glasgow from Toronto are offered by Air Transat, while Westjet has seasonal flights from Edinburgh to Calgary, Halifax and Toronto. Several airlines, including United and JetBlue, fly from various cities in the United States to both Glasgow and Edinburgh. Flights from a variety of US hubs route flights via London or Amsterdam.

From Australia and New Zealand. Qantas offers non-direct flights from Sydney and Melbourne to London. Air New Zealand has daily flights to London from Auckland.

From England and Republic of Ireland. There are direct services from all parts of the UK with British Airways, easyJet and Ryanair, including frequent departures from Birmingham, Heathrow, Gatwick, Luton, Stansted, Southampton, Bristol, Newcastle and Manchester. Aer Lingus and Ryanair have regular flights from Dublin.

From Europe. Most major European airlines, including budget airlines Ryanair and easyJet, have direct flights from continental Europe to Glasgow, Edinburgh or Aberdeen.

Air fares. The highest air fares are from June to September, and during holiday periods, especially Christmas and the New Year; fares in other months of the year may be considerably lower, but in any case, the further in advance you book, the cheaper the fare.

From the US, a direct flight to London with a domestic flight to either Glasgow or Edinburgh likely to be the cheapest option. Many American airlines offer a variety of package deals, both for group travel and for those who wish to travel independently. Packages include airfare, accommodation and travel between holiday destinations and may include some meals.

By rail. The train journey from London King's Cross to Edinburgh takes 4hr 30min, and from London Euston to Glasgow 5hr. A sleeper service is available from London Euston to Glasgow, Edinburgh, Aberdeen, Inverness and Fort William.

Visitors can take advantage of a variety of special fare plans that operate in Scotland. The **Spirit of Scotland Travelpass** is available for either 4 days of travel over 8 consecutive days (£149), or 8 days of travel over 15 consecutive days (£189). The pass gives unlimited travel on many bus routes and Caledonian MacBrayne (CalMac; www.calmac.co.uk) ferries as well as on Scotland's rail network. Travelpass holders can obtain a 20 percent reduction on NorthLink sailings from Aberdeen or Stromness to Orkney and Shetland. It can be purchased at ScotRail stations or online (www.scotrail.co.uk), and at selected English travel centres. You can also choose from a selection of Rail Rover tickets; enquire at railway stations.

Visitors from abroad who wish to tour by rail can buy a **BritRail Pass** (www.britrail.net) before leaving their home countries. These offer unlimited travel on the railway network throughout Scotland, England and Wales during a consecutive period of 3, 4, 8, 15, 22 days, or a month. The **Flexipass** allows journeys to be made on non-consecutive days; for example, 4 days unlimited travel over a month period. Children aged 5–15 pay half-price. The **BritRail Youth Pass** is for youngsters aged 16–25. None of these can be purchased in Britain.

By road. From London the quickest route is to take the M1 north to connect with the A1. If you are in the west, the M5 merges with the M6 and connects with the M74 to Glasgow.

To take your own car to Scotland, you will need proof of ownership and insurance documents, including Green Card insurance.

There are frequent coach services from all over Britain to various Scottish destinations by **National Express** (www.nationalexpress.com) and **Scottish Citylink** (www.citylink.co.uk).

By sea. Ferry services from Northern Ireland operate from Larne and Belfast to Cairnryan near Stranraer.

GUIDES AND TOURS

Dozens of bus tours are available in Scotland. Timberbush Tours (www.timberbush-tours.co.uk), based in Edinburgh, offers multi-choice tours to St Andrews, Loch Lomond, Loch Ness, the Borders and other destinations; Gray Line (www.graylinescotland.com) and Glasgow-based Scottish Tours (www.scottishtours.co.uk) offer similar options. All tours can be booked through the tourist information offices, at Waverley Mall in Edinburgh and George Square in Glasgow. Tour operators, centres and hotels provide package holidays for sports such as golf and other outdoor sports.

Both Glasgow and Edinburgh have a number of city hop-on-hop-off bus tours. Tours originate at George Square in Glasgow (www.city-sightseeing.com) and at Waverley Bridge in Edinburgh (www.hop-on-hop-off-bus.com/edinburgh-bus-tours).

Details of guides and tours can also be obtained from The Secretary, Scottish Tour Guides Association, Norrie's House, 18b Broad Street, Stirling, FK8 1EF, www.stga.co.uk. Members of this association wear official badges engraved with their names. Most are based in Edinburgh, Glasgow, Aberdeen and Dundee. Some will accompany tours.

H

HEALTH AND MEDICAL CARE

Scotland, home of much pioneering work in medicine, is proud of the high standard of its health care. Medical care is free for EU (on production of the EHIC card) and Commonwealth residents under the National Health Service

(NHS). Other nationals should check to be sure they have adequate health insurance coverage. US residents should be aware that Medicare does not apply outside the United States.

Emergency care. Major hospitals with 24hr emergency service are: Edinburgh Royal Infirmary, tel: 0131-536 1000; Glasgow Royal Infirmary, tel: 0141-211 4000; Aberdeen Royal Infirmary, tel: 0345-456 6000; and Inverness Raigmore, tel: 01463-704000.

Pharmacies. In Edinburgh, Glasgow and a few other major centres you should find a duty chemist (drugstore) open until 9pm; otherwise, contact a police station for help in filling in an emergency prescription, or dial 999.

Insects. In the summer, midges are a nuisance or worse, especially on Scotland's west coast. Clegs (horse flies) and tiny but devilish berry bugs also attack in warmer weather. Insect repellents aren't always effective; ask the advice of a chemist.

Scottish/Gaelic **English**
aber **river mouth**
Auld Reekie **Edinburgh (Old Smoky)**
ben **mountain**
bide a wee **wait a bit**
biggin **building**
brae **hillside**
bramble **blackberry**
brig **bridge**
burn **stream**
cairn **pile of stones as landmark**
ceilidh **song/story gathering**
clachan **hamlet**
croft **small land-holding**
dinna fash yersel' **don't get upset**
eilean **island**

L

LANGUAGE

Gaelic and old Scottish words and phrases in everyday use will baffle the most fluent English speaker. Today, just over 60,000 Scots speak Gaelic, most of them residents of the Western Isles. English spoken with a strong Scots accent can take a while to get used to, and place names are often not pronounced the way you'd expect them to be: Kirkcudbright is *Kircoobree*, Culzean is *Cullane*, Colquhoun is *Cohoon*, Culross is *Coorus*, Menzies is *Mingies*, Dalziell is *Dee-ell*.

LGBTQ+ TRAVELLERS

Scotland is a largely conservative country and the LGBTQ+ scene is found primarily in Edinburgh and Glasgow, both of which have a lively gay nightlife scene. The centre of Edinburgh's gay community is Broughton Street at the east end of town. Support is offered by the LGBT Helpline Scotland (www.lgbt-helpline-scotland.org.uk). The monthly magazine *Scotsgay* has a useful website (www.scotsgay.co.uk).

M

MAPS

Most tourist offices dispense street maps for free, as well as regional maps, though for getting around major towns and cities, a GPS-enabled smartphone or navigation app is hard to beat. Collins also publishes illustrated street maps of Edinburgh and Glasgow and the *A–Z Street Atlas* is available for both cities.

If you're planning a walk of more than a couple of hours in duration, or intend to walk in the Scottish hills at all, it is strongly recommended that you carry the relevant **Ordnance Survey** or OS (www.ordnancesurvey.co.uk) map, which are renowned for their accuracy and clarity; they come in two series: the pink Landranger (1:50,000) and the orange Explorer (1:25,000).

fell **hill**
firth **estuary**
gait **street**
ghillie **attendant to hunting or fishing**
glen **valley**
haud yer wheesht **shut up**
inver **mouth of river**
ken **know**
kirk **church**
kyle **strait, narrows**
lang may yer lum reek **long may your chimney smoke (i.e. may
    you have a long life)**
link **dune**
linn **waterfall**
loch **lake**
mickle **small amount**
mull **promontory**
ness **headland**
provost **mayor**
sett **tartan pattern**
skirl **shriek of bagpipes**
strath **river valley**
thunderplump **thunderstorm**
tollbooth **old courthouse/jail**
wynd **lane, alley**

MEDIA

Television: Viewers in Scotland have plenty of choice with two main BBC channels and several commercial channels. Digital television services provide a wide range of extra channels. Many larger hotels offer a variety of cable and satellite TV channels and pay-per-view films.

Radio: Radio Scotland is the main BBC radio service and national BBC radio stations also operate in Scotland. A range of commercial radio stations cater for different areas of Scotland. Various international stations can also be received.

Newspapers and magazines: In addition to British national newspapers, Scottish daily papers are: the *Herald* (published in Glasgow), the *Scotsman* (published in Edinburgh), the *Daily Record*, and the *Aberdeen Press and Journal*. Details of events and entertainment in and around Glasgow and Edinburgh are given in the magazine *The List* (www.list.co.uk), published every two months. *The New York Times International Edition* and *US weekly* news magazines are sold in the major centres and at airports.

MONEY

Currency. The pound sterling (£) is a decimal monetary unit and is divided into 100 pence (p). Coins consist of 1p, 2p, 5p, 10p, 20p, 50p, £1 and £2; and banknotes consist of £5, £10, £20 and £50.

Scottish banks issue their own notes, which are legal tender in England and Wales, although some shops south of the border may refuse to accept them; English banks will readily change them for you.

Currency exchange. You will get the best exchange rate for your foreign currency at banks (see Opening hours); currency exchange bureaux rarely offer as good a rate, and you'll get the worst rate at your hotel.

Credit/debit cards. Major credit and debit cards are widely accepted in hotels, restaurants, petrol stations and shops, although not always in small guesthouses and B&Bs – signs are usually displayed indicating which cards are accepted.

Travellers' cheques. Travellers' cheques are accepted throughout Scotland. You'll need your passport when cashing them, and banks will charge a fee. The American Express office will cash its own travellers' cheques without a fee.

O

OPENING HOURS

Opening hours may vary from place to place. However, **banks** are usually open

Monday–Friday 9am–5pm, with branches in city centres open on Saturday mornings. Banks in small towns may close for lunch. Some rural areas are served only by mobile banks that arrive at regular intervals and stay for a few hours.

Offices and businesses are usually open Monday–Friday 9am–5pm; some have Saturday hours.

Post offices are generally open Monday–Friday 9am–5.30pm and Saturday 9am–12.30pm. Sub-stations sometimes have a half-day closing on Wednesday or Thursday.

Shop hours are normally Monday–Saturday 9am–5.30pm, some until 7pm or 8pm on Thursday. Some shops in villages and smaller towns close on Sunday and may close for lunch. In the larger cities in major shopping areas, shops open at either 11am or noon on Sunday and close at 5pm or 5.30pm.

Museums and sightseeing attractions have greatly varying opening hours. As a rule, attractions are open from about 9.30am until late afternoon, or early evening in summer. In winter many castles and other places of interest are closed to the public or open for limited periods. It's best to call for information. Museums in the cities are generally open Monday–Saturday 10am–5pm and noon–5pm on Sunday.

Major **tourist information offices** are open all year round, usually Monday–Saturday 9am–6/7pm and Sunday 10am–5/6pm in July and August. At other times of the year, they close earlier.

P

POLICE

Most Scottish police wear chest guards and carry batons, though regular street officers do not carry guns. Police patrol cars usually have yellow stripes and a blue light.

The emergency telephone number for police aid is **999** all over the country. You can also dial 0 and ask for the police.

POST OFFICES

Letters and packages sent within the UK can use the first- or second-class postal service. Because second-class mail may be slow, it's advisable to pay the modest extra postage for first class. Postcards and letters to Europe and elsewhere overseas automatically go by airmail. The post office offers an express mail service, Parcelforce Worldwide.

Stamps are sold at post offices (found in almost every Scottish village even if they share space with grocery shops) and newsagents, as well as from vending machines. Postboxes are red and come in many shapes and sizes.

Edinburgh's main post office is in Waverley Mall Shopping Centre, Waverley Bridge. Glasgow's main post office is at 136 West Nile Street.

Postage: within the UK from £1.25 first-class, 76p second-class; to Europe and the rest of world, airmail from £1.55.

PUBLIC HOLIDAYS

Bank holidays in Scotland are not always closing days for offices and shops. Many towns have their individual holidays, generally on a Monday. If a public holiday falls on a Saturday or Sunday, it is usual to take off the following Monday.

1 January **New Year's Day**

2 January **Bank Holiday**

30 November **St Andrew's Day**

25 December **Christmas Day**

26 December **Boxing Day**

Moveable dates:

March or April **Good Friday**

May **Spring Bank Holiday**

August **Summer Bank Holiday**

TELEPHONES

With the ubiquity of mobiles, there are now few public phone boxes/kiosks. Those that do exist usually accept coins, phonecards or credit/debit cards; phonecards of various denominations can be purchased from newsagents, post offices and tourist information offices. Some phones in small towns and public buildings are still coin-operated only.

Public phone booths display information on overseas dialling codes and the international exchange. Dial 118 505 for international directory inquiries, 155 for an international operator. Local directory enquiries are provided by several companies – numbers include 118 500, 118 365, 118 212 and 118 118, and for operator assistance, dial 100. Note that all 118 services are very expensive. To make a local reverse-charge call, dial 100 and ask the operator to reverse the charges.

Mobile (cell) phone coverage is as good in Scotland as the rest of the UK, and all the main UK networks cover the Highlands and Islands, though you'll still find many places in among the hills or out on the islands where there's no signal at all. Coverage varies extensively between different mobile phone companies. If you have a GSM phone the roaming charges may well be high, hence the cheapest option is to buy a local UK SIM card; incoming calls will be free and local calls inexpensive. Check out all the options before travelling.

TIME ZONES

Scotland, like the rest of the United Kingdom, is on Greenwich Mean Time. Between April and October clocks are put forward one hour.

New York	**Edinburgh**	Jo'burg	Sydney	Auckland
7am	**noon**	1pm	9pm	11pm

TIPPING

While tipping is customary in Scotland, there's no pressure. Hotels and restaurants may add a service charge to your bill, in which case tipping is not really necessary. If service is not included, add about 10 percent to your bill. Many cafés and informal restaurants have a box for tips beside the cash register.

Tip hotel porters about £1 per bag, and tip your hotel maid around £5 per week. Lavatory attendants should get 20–50p. Your taxi driver will be pleased with 10 percent, and so will your tour guide. Hairdressers should get around 10–20 percent.

TOURIST INFORMATION

The official tourist board is known as **VisitScotland** (www.visitscotland.com), though it has recently axed many of its tourist offices; instead, there are now 26 iCentres (identified by purple signs with an iCentre in white), effectively regional visitor centres that dispense information on the surrounding area (and invariably beyond). In addition, you'll find the occasional local, independent tourist office, as well as information centres in the national parks.

In Edinburgh the **Tourist Information Centre** is at 249 High Street, and in Glasgow, it's at 156/158 Buchanan Street.

The national headquarters of **VisitScotland** (www.visitscotland.com) is at Ocean Point One, 94 Ocean Drive, Edinburgh (tel: 0131-524 2121) but only written and telephone inquiries are accepted here. For further information on Scotland and the rest of Britain check www.visitbritain.com. In London you can drop into the City of London Visitor Centre, St Paul's Churchyard, London EC4M 8BY; tel: 020-7332 1456.

TRANSPORT

Scotland's extensive public transport network can be of considerable use to tourists. If you're touring the north without a car, a Travelpass (see page 122) enables you to travel on most coaches, trains and ferries operating in the Highlands and Islands at a significant saving. Maps, timetables and brochures are available free from tourist offices and transport terminals (see page 131). There are also money-saving excursions, weekend and island-to-island ferry schemes.

City transport. Most Scottish towns and cities have good bus services, particularly Edinburgh and Glasgow, which also have night services. Family and other discount tickets are available in Edinburgh at the Lothian Buses offices at Waverley Bridge, Hanover Street and Haymarket (www.lothianbuses.com). The First Bus (www.firstgroup.com/ukbus/scotland_east) company serves urban and rural areas around Edinburgh. In Glasgow, the main bus company is First Bus (www.firstgroup.com/greater-glasgow); contact the Travel Centre at Buchanan bus station, Killermont Street.

Edinburgh Trams (www.edinburghtrams.com), which works in partnership with Lothian Buses, runs one line from the airport to Newhaven via the city centre.

Glasgow also has a simple but efficient subway system, nicknamed 'the Clockwork Orange', which operates in the city centre. The Park and Ride scheme involves parking your car at certain underground stations on the outskirts of the city and then taking the subway into the centre.

Coaches. Comfortable and rapid long-distance coaches with toilets link the major towns. For details, visit the websites of **National Express** (www.nationalexpress.com) and **Scottish Citylink** (www.citylink.co.uk). Citylink offers the Explorer Pass for three days' travel out of five (£45), five days' travel out of ten (£74) or eight days' travel out of 16 (£99), good on both major and local routes.

Trains. Train services include the InterCity trains, with principal routes from London to Glasgow's Central Station (5hr) and to Edinburgh's Waverley Station (4hr 30min); there are day and night trains. From Glasgow's Queen Street Station, routes continue on to Perth, Dundee, Aberdeen and Inverness and there are smaller, secondary lines. For **National Rail Enquiries**, visit www.nationalrail.co.uk.

Ferries. Ferries to the Western Isles are run by **Caledonian MacBrayne** (www.calmac.co.uk), while NorthLink Ferries (www.northlinkferries.co.uk) connects the mainland with Orkney and Shetland; there are ferry services from Aberdeen to Kirkwall and Lerwick, and from Scrabster to Stromness. There are also many ferries between the islands. Reservations are essential in peak season if you are travelling with a vehicle.

Taxis. In Scotland's major centres you'll find most taxis are the black, London-style cabs. A taxi's yellow 'For Hire' sign is lit when it's available for hire. There are taxi ranks at airports and stations, and you can hail them on the street. Major centres have 24hr radio taxi services. There's an extra charge for luggage. If you hire a taxi for a long-distance trip, negotiate the price with the driver before setting off.

V

VISAS AND ENTRY REQUIREMENTS

For non-British citizens the same formalities apply at Scottish ports of entry as elsewhere in the UK. Citizens of EU countries need only an identity card. Visitors from the US and most Commonwealth countries need only a valid passport for stays of up to six months.

On arrival at a British port or airport, if you have goods to declare you follow the red channel; with nothing to declare you take the green route, bypassing inspection, although customs officers may make random spot checks. Free exchange of non-duty-free goods for personal use is permitted between EU countries and the UK. Duty-free items are still subject to restrictions: check before you go. There's no limit on the amount of currency you can bring into or take out of Britain.

W

WEBSITES AND INTERNET ACCESS

The following are some useful websites for planning your visit.

www.visitbritain.com British Tourist Authority

https://peoplemakeglasgow.com Greater Glasgow and Clyde Valley

www.edinburgh.org Comprehensive guide to the capital

www.historicenvironment.scot Caring for and promoting Scotland's historic environment

www.nts.org.uk National Trust for Scotland

www.undiscoveredscotland.co.uk Undiscovered Scotland

www.visitscotland.com VisitScotland

Scotland is well serviced when it comes to internet access, with wi-fi available at nearly all accommodation, even in the Highlands and Islands. Most cafés, restaurants and pubs will also have wi-fi, though you will of course be obliged to make a purchase. Otherwise, public libraries across Scotland offer free internet access.

Y

YOUTH HOSTELS

Hostelling Scotland (www.hostellngscotland.org.uk) – formerly The Scottish Youth Hostels Association – runs around 60 hostels across the mainland and throughout the islands. Visitors can stay without being members of the association but membership brings many benefits, including reduced prices for rooms. Breakfast is not normally included in the price, though most hostels have self-catering facilities. In addition there are plenty of independent hostels across Scotland.

WHERE TO STAY

Accommodation around Scotland covers a wide spectrum, from the basic B&B (bed-and-breakfast) to modern luxury hotels and ancient refurbished castles. VisitScotland (www.visitscotland.com) publishes many brochures and booklets detailing available accommodation, prices, facilities, etc.

Below, you will find a selection of accommodation chosen for its quality and value for money. Prices are based on two people sharing a double room with breakfast in high season. Keep in mind that prices vary according to time of year and availability. All rooms have bath or shower, and all establishments take major credit and debit cards unless otherwise indicated. Edinburgh is extremely busy during the Edinburgh Festival (August), so book well in advance if you plan to visit the capital during that period.

££££	over £250
£££	£150–£250
££	£100–£150
£	below £100

EDINBURGH

The Balmoral ££££ *1 Princes St, EH2 2EQ,* www.roccofortehotels.com. In a commanding position at the east end of Princes Street, this grand hotel has long been a legend, with luxury at every turn. It also has a distinguished restaurant in *Number One*. 168 rooms.

The Glasshouse Hotel £££ *2 Greenside Place, EH1 3AA,* www.theglasshouse hotel.co.uk. Situated near the east end of Princes Street, this is a state-of-the-art building where the rooms surround a two-acre (0.8-hectare) roof garden scattered with Philippe Starck furniture. The exterior rooms have splendid views to the New Town or across the Firth of Forth. 77 rooms.

Ibis Edinburgh Centre South Bridge ££ *77 South Bridge, EH1 1HN,* www.all. accor.com. Well located close to the Royal Mile, this is not just another chain hotel; the decor is impeccable and the rooms have extremely comfortable beds. There's also a 24hr bar. 259 rooms.

The Inn on the Mile £££ *82 High Street, EH1 1LL*, www.theinnonthemile. co.uk. You'll find boutique-style bedrooms with attention to detail and comfort to the fore in this lovely old pub, just a short walk from the castle. You can even enjoy live music between Thurs and Sun. 9 rooms.

Kimpton Charlotte Square ££££ *38 Charlotte Square, EH2 4HQ*, www. kimptoncharlotte-square.com. Situated on Edinburgh's grandest square, this graceful Georgian building conceals magnificently appointed rooms, while breakfast is taken in the stunning inner courtyard. 198 rooms.

Radisson Collection Royal Mile ££££ *1 George Bridge 1V, EH1 1AD*, www. radissonhotels.com. Perfectly placed on Edinburgh's Royal Mile, this splendid luxurious boutique hotel certainly has the wow factor. Fabulous design and stunning use of bold textiles. 136 rooms.

Waldorf Astoria – The Caledonian ££££ *Princes Street, EH1 2AB*, www. hilton. One of the city's landmarks, this traditional luxury hotel is at the western end of bustling Princes Street, with views of Edinburgh Castle. A pool, sauna and steam room are complemented by a fine restaurant serving modern Scottish cuisine. 241 rooms.

SOUTHEAST AND THE BORDERS

Burts Hotel £££ *Market Square, Melrose, TD6 9PN*, www.burtshotel.co.uk. This family-run hotel is housed in a restored 1722 town house near the abbey. Rooms are airy and restful, and the dining room serves good traditional Scottish food. 20 rooms.

Ednam House Hotel ££ *Bridge Street, Kelso, TD5 7HT*, www.ednamhouse. com. This large hotel on the River Tweed is housed in a mid-eighteenth-century Georgian house, its rooms boasting antiques and period furnishings. You can feast on good Scottish food while admiring the view of the river from the dining room. Golf and salmon fishing, cycling paths and walks are all available close by. 33 rooms.

Greywalls ££££ *Duncur Road, Muirfield, Gullane, East Lothian, EH31 2EG,* www.greywalls.co.uk. On the edge of the Muirfield championship golf course, this attractive Edwardian house was designed by noted architect Sir Edwin Lutyens, with gardens laid out by Gertrude Jekyll. With fine views and an award-winning restaurant, it is a 40min drive from the centre of Edinburgh. 23 rooms.

Hundalee House ££ *Jedburgh, TD8 6PA,* www.accommodation-scotland.org. This charming house is set in fifteen acres (six hectares) and perfect for touring the Borders region and just a mile from Jedburgh. You are guaranteed a warm welcome from the owners who have run this B&B for more than 35 years. 4 rooms.

Knockinaam Lodge ££££ *Portpatrick, Dumfries and Galloway, DG9 9AD,* www.knockinaamlodge.com. Chic hunting-lodge-style Victorian hotel set in beautiful parkland with immaculately presented rooms. Fine sea views, excellent cuisine, fishing and superb walking. 10 rooms.

GLASGOW

ABode Glasgow ££ *129 Bath Street, G2 2SZ,* www.abodeglasgow.co.uk. Located in an elegant Edwardian building, the decor reflects the city's modern renaissance, beautifully combining traditional features with boutique design and modern comforts. 59 rooms.

Argyll Guest House ££ *970 Sauchiehall Street, G3 7TH,* www.argyllguest houseglasgow.co.uk. Near Kelvingrove Park and the art galleries, this small, friendly hotel is a good budget option whose staff are very helpful. 18 rooms.

Carlton George £££ *44 West George Street, G2 1DH,* www.carlton.nl. A modern, luxurious, state-of-the-art hotel in the heart of Glasgow with a wide selection of rooms in five categories. The *Windows* rooftop restaurant offers excellent Scottish cooking and great views. 64 rooms.

Grasshoppers Hotel ££ *87 Union Street, G1 3TA,* www.grasshoppersglasgow. com. Penthouse rooms above an office building, close to the historic Glasgow Central station. Unsurprisingly, it offers great city views. It's wonderfully quiet here for its central location, and friendly staff and a wholesome breakfast make this a unique city experience. 30 rooms.

Malmaison ££ *278 West George Street, G2 4LL,* www.malmaison.com. Modern and trendy with beautifully decorated rooms, this former Greek Orthodox church still manages to preserve its important historical character. Vaulted cellar restaurant serving Scottish flavours with a French influence. 72 rooms.

Hotel du Vin & Bistro £££ *1 Devonshire Gardens, G12 0UX,* www.hotelduvin. com. In a leafy district west of the centre, this luxury boutique hotel occupies a stunning Victorian terrace and offers beautifully decorated rooms – some with four-poster and hot tubs – and impeccable service. 49 rooms.

CENTRAL SCOTLAND

Apex City Quay Hotel and Spa ££ *1 West Victoria Dock Road, Dundee, DD1 3JP,* www.apexhotels.co.uk. Located in the heart of the City Quay development and overlooking the River Tay, this striking hotel is stylish and contemporary. Good food, plus spa, sauna and treatment rooms. 151 rooms.

Dalmunzie Castle Hotel £££ *Spittal o' Glenshee, Blairgowrie, PH10 7QG,* www. dalmunzieestate.com. A mountain laird's mansion with splendid views, situated eighteen miles (29km) north of Blairgowrie on the A93. Rooms of all descriptions, including Tower Rooms, plus self-catering cottages. Excellent nine-hole golf course, and conveniently located for the ski slopes. 17 rooms.

Dunfallandy House ££ *Pitlochry, PH16 5NA,* www.dunfallandyhouse.co.uk. Just two miles (3km) south of Pitlochry, this Georgian house overlooks the town and has stunning views of the Tummel Valley. Impeccably kept rooms are complemented by public areas including lounge and dining area, plus extensive gardens. 8 rooms.

The George Hotel ££ *Main Street East, Inveraray PA32 8TT,* www.thegeorge hotel.co.uk. *The George* has been sensitively restored, its dog-friendly rooms replete with fine antiques and paintings a star feature. With flagstone flooring, log fires and dimly lit nooks and crannies, the pub part is a terrific spot for a bite to eat or a drink. 17 rooms.

Killiecrankie House £££ *Killiecrankie, Pitlochry, Perthshire*, www.killiecrankie house.co.uk. Five gorgeously furnished rooms, each with a four-poster bed and freestanding bath. The price includes dinner and a gourmet breakfast cooked by an award-winning chef. 5 rooms.

Mercure Aberdeen Caledonian £ *10–14 Union Terrace, Aberdeen, AB10 1WE*, www.all.accor.com. Centrally located Victorian building with modern facilities and elegant public rooms; restaurant and café/wine bar. 83 rooms.

The Old Course Hotel ££££ *St Andrews, Fife KY16 9SP*, www.oldcoursehotel. co.uk. Modern luxury hotel bordering the historic golf course with good restaurants, indoor swimming pool, health spa and beauty salon. 109 rooms and 35 suites.

Colessio ££ *33 Spittal Street, Stirling, FK8 1DU*, www.hotelcolessio.com. Superbly positioned in the heart of the Old Town, this magnificent Georgian building was formerly a bank and then the city's Royal Infirmary; the rooms here come in four different categories, and there's also a quality restaurant. 40 rooms.

The Royal George Hotel ££ *Tay Street, Perth, RH1 5LD*, www.theroyalgeorge hotel.co.uk. Beautifully located on the banks of the River Tay, The Royal George has been receiving visitors for over 240 years. Enjoy a traditional breakfast in the conservatory with fine views of the river. 45 rooms.

HIGHLANDS AND ISLANDS

The Arisaig Hotel ££ *Main Road, Arisaig, Inverness-shire, PH39 4NH*, www. arisaighotel.co.uk. *Arisaig Hotel* dates back to the Jacobite era, and was originally built as a coaching inn around 1720. The hotel looks across Arisaig Bay towards the isles of Eigg and Muck. Enjoy good food and great music in the lively *Crofter's Rest* bar. 13 rooms.

Bosville Hotel £££ *Bosville Terrace, Portree, Skye, IV51 9DG*, www.perlehotels. com. Stylish accommodation with views of Portree Harbour and Cuillin Hills; sleek rooms with lots of vintage touches and an outstanding bistro (see page 113). 20 rooms.

The Bracken Hide ££££ *Struan Road, Portree,* www.brackenhide.co.uk. On the western fringes of Portree, this wilderness lodge turned heads on the hotel scene when it opened in 2023. Designed to blend in with the landscape, the stone-built main lodge and wooden cabins are scattered across 52 acres (21 hectares) of untamed land. Elsewhere, you'll find a whisky room, restaurant, sauna and wild swimming pond. 27 cabins.

CARTER'S REST £££ *8/9 Upper Milovaig, 4 miles west of Colbost,* www.carters restskye.co.uk. Antique furniture, super-king beds dressed with butter-soft linen and a sprinkling of little touches like a digital radio, combine to great effect in this luxury four-star B&B. There's an inviting guest lounge with a wood-burner and soul-soothing coast views, and a glass-fronted sauna overlooking Loch Pooltiel. 3 rooms, 1 apartment.

Craigmonie Hotel ££ *9 Annfield Road, Inverness, IV2 3HX,* www.craigmonie hotelinverness.co.uk. Situated in the heart of Inverness with the feel of a country dwelling, *Craigmonie* offers luxurious leisure activities and a delicious à la carte menu. 40 rooms.

Culloden House Hotel ££££ *Culloden, Inverness, IV1 7BZ,* www.culloden house.co.uk. Georgian house close to the site of the 1746 battle, and three miles (5km) east of Inverness on the A96, and where Bonnie Prince Charlie slept before the battle. Some of the rooms have crystal chandeliers and a marble fireplace. Extensive gardens and parkland include a tennis court and croquet lawn. 28 rooms.

Inverlochy Castle ££££ *Torlundy, Fort William, PH33 6SN,* www.inverlochy castlehotel.com. Luxury Victorian castle three miles (5km) northeast of Fort William on A82. Set in fifty acres (20 hectares) of woodland with splendid views of the loch and mountains. Fine cuisine, fishing, and watersports on the loch. 17 rooms.

Kinloch Lodge ££££ *Sleat, Skye, IV43 8QY,* www.kinloch-lodge.co.uk. The home of the chief of Clan Macdonald and his wife, the manor has been expanded from a 1680 hunting lodge and contains family portraits and clan mementos. The wonderful food is based on traditional Scottish cuisine made with local ingredients. 15 rooms.

Lickisto Blackhouse Camping ££ *Lickisto (Liceasto)*, www.lickistoblackhousecamping.co.uk. Beautiful campsite by a rocky bay with a restored blackhouse for campers' use. A couple of renovated thatched byres shelter basic washing facilities, while the blackhouse is the place to cook, eat and mingle by the peat fire. There is a selection of other accommodation, from an old cattle byre turned snug bothy to a fire-warmed bell tent and a handful of yurts with double beds. 1 bell tent, 1 bothy plus campervan/tent pitches.

The Moorings Hotel ££ *Banavie, Fort William, PH33 7LY*, www.moorings-fortwilliam.co.uk. By the Caledonian Canal, the hotel has views of Ben Nevis, while some rooms have balconies overlooking the canal itself. Excellent restaurant, café and bars. 36 rooms.

Scarista House £££ *Isle of Harris, Western Isles, HS3 3HX*, www.scaristahouse.com. This Georgian manse is set in a remote area overlooking a beach – perfect for getting away from it all. All rooms have sea views, and there's an outstanding restaurant too. 6 rooms.

Summer Isles Hotel £££ *Achiltibuie, Ross-shire, IV26 2YG*, www.summerisleshotel.com. Over the years the hotel has established itself as an oasis of civilisation hidden away in a stunningly beautiful but still wild and untouched landscape. Nearly everything you eat here is home-produced or locally caught. 14 rooms.

Tiroran House £££ *Mull, PA69 6ES (off the road to Iona on the B8035)*, www.tiroran.com. This lovely country house is tucked away in beautiful grounds with spacious lawns and gardens on the shore of Loch Scridain. Its public rooms and comfortable bedrooms are more like those in a home than a hotel. Good food is served in an elegant setting. Telephone for directions before you set off, or you'll run the risk of getting lost. 10 rooms plus self-catering cottages.

Western Isles Hotel ££ *Tobermory, Mull, PA75 6PR*, www.westernisleshotel.co.uk. A welcoming atmosphere greets visitors at this traditional hotel with spectacular views over the Sound of Mull and Tobermory Bay. The food is excellent and served in three different dining rooms, including the charming conservatory with lovely views. 28 rooms.

INDEX

THE **MINI** ROUGH GUIDE TO
SCOTLAND

First Edition 2024

Editors: Joanna Reeves, Beth Williams
Authors: Alice Fellows, Jackie Staddon and Hilary Weston
Updater: Norm Longley
Picture Editor: Tom Smyth
Cartography Update: Carte
Layout: Pradeep Thapliyal
Head of DTP and Pre-Press: Rebeka Davies
Head of Publishing: Sarah Clark
Photography Credits: David Cruickshanks/Apa Publications 24, 30, 41, 47; Douglas Macgilvray/Apa Publications 19; Glasgow Life 49; iStock 4TC, 4TL, 4ML, 7T, 22, 107; Leonardo 7B; Mockford & Bonetti/Apa Publications 4TC, 6T, 6B, 15, 26, 28, 31, 33, 35, 36, 37, 38, 44, 45, 51, 53, 57, 95, 98; National Galleries of Scotland 20; Public domain 17; Shutterstock 1, 4MC, 4ML, 5T, 5M, 5M, 12, 48, 54, 75, 78, 80, 83, 84, 85
Cover Credits: Cottage on Glencoe **Helen Hotson**/Shutterstock

Distribution

UK, Ireland and Europe: Apa Publications (UK) Ltd; sales@roughguides.com
United States and Canada: Ingram Publisher Services; ips@ingramcontent.com
Australia and New Zealand: Booktopia; retailer@booktopia.com.au
Worldwide: Apa Publications (UK) Ltd; sales@roughguides.com

Special Sales, Content Licensing and CoPublishing

Rough Guides can be purchased in bulk quantities at discounted prices. We can create special editions, personalised jackets and corporate imprints tailored to your needs. sales@roughguides.com; http://roughguides.com

All Rights Reserved
© 2024 Apa Digital AG
License edition © Apa Publications Ltd UK

Printed in Czech Republic

This book was produced using **Typefi** automated publishing software.

Contact us

Every effort has been made to provide accurate information in this publication, but changes are inevitable. The publisher cannot be held responsible for any resulting loss, inconvenience or injury sustained by any traveller as a result of information or advice contained in the guide. We would appreciate it if readers would call our attention to any errors or outdated information, or if you feel we've left something out. Please send your comments with the subject line "Rough Guide Mini Scotland Update" to mail@uk.roughguides.com.